Reference Architectures
Complete Self-Assessment Guide

The guidance in this Self-Assessment is based on Reference Architectures best practices and standards in business process architecture, design and quality management. The guidance is also based on the professional judgment of the individual collaborators listed in the Acknowledgments.

Notice of rights

You are licensed to use the Self-Assessment contents in your presentations and materials for internal use and customers without asking us - we are here to help.

All rights reserved for the book itself: this book may not be reproduced or transmitted in any form by any means, electronic, mechanical, photocopying, recording, or otherwise, without the prior written permission of the publisher.

The information in this book is distributed on an "As Is" basis without warranty. While every precaution has been taken in the preparation of he book, neither the author nor the publisher shall have any liability to any person or entity with respect to any loss or damage caused or alleged to be caused directly or indirectly by the instructions contained in this book or by the products described in it.

Trademarks

Many of the designations used by manufacturers and sellers to distinguish their products are claimed as trademarks. Where those designations appear in this book, and the publisher was aware of a trademark claim, the designations appear as requested by the owner of the trademark. All other product names and services identified throughout this book are used in editorial fashion only and for the benefit of such companies with no intention of infringement of the trademark. No such use, or the use of any trade name, is intended to convey endorsement or other affiliation with this book.

Copyright © by The Art of Service
http://theartofservice.com
service@theartofservice.com

Table of Contents

About The Art of Service

The Art of Service, Business Process Architects since 2000, is dedicated to helping stakeholders achieve excellence.

Defining, designing, creating, and implementing a process to solve a stakeholders challenge or meet an objective is the most valuable role… In EVERY group, company, organization and department.

Unless you're talking a one-time, single-use project, there should be a process. Whether that process is managed and implemented by humans, AI, or a combination of the two, it needs to be designed by someone with a complex enough perspective to ask the right questions.

Someone capable of asking the right questions and step back and say, 'What are we really trying to accomplish here? And is there a different way to look at it?'

With The Art of Service's Standard Requirements Self-Assessments, we empower people who can do just that — whether their title is marketer, entrepreneur, manager, salesperson, consultant, Business Process Manager, executive assistant, IT Manager, CIO etc... —they are the people who rule the future. They are people who watch the process as it happens, and ask the right questions to make the process work better.

Contact us when you need any support with this Self-Assessment and any help with templates, blue-prints and examples of standard documents you might need:

http://theartofservice.com
service@theartofservice.com

Included Resources - how to access

Included with your purchase of the book is the Reference

Architectures Self-Assessment Spreadsheet Dashboard which contains all questions and Self-Assessment areas and auto-generates insights, graphs, and project RACI planning - all with examples to get you started right away.

How? Simply send an email to
access@theartofservice.com
with this books' title in the subject to get the Reference Architectures Self Assessment Tool right away.

You will receive the following contents with New and Updated specific criteria:

- The latest quick edition of the book in PDF

- The latest complete edition of the book in PDF, which criteria correspond to the criteria in...

- The Self-Assessment Excel Dashboard, and...

- Example pre-filled Self-Assessment Excel Dashboard to get familiar with results generation

- In-depth specific Checklists covering the topic

- Project management checklists and templates to assist with implementation

INCLUDES LIFETIME SELF ASSESSMENT UPDATES

Every self assessment comes with Lifetime Updates and Lifetime Free Updated Books. Lifetime Updates is an industry-first feature which allows you to receive verified self assessment updates, ensuring you always have the most accurate information at your fingertips.

Get it now- you will be glad you did - do it now, before you forget.

Send an email to **access@theartofservice.com** with this books' title in the subject to get the Reference Architectures Self Assessment Tool right away.

Purpose of this Self-Assessment

This Self-Assessment has been developed to improve understanding of the requirements and elements of Reference Architectures, based on best practices and standards in business process architecture, design and quality management.

It is designed to allow for a rapid Self-Assessment to determine how closely existing management practices and procedures correspond to the elements of the Self-Assessment.

The criteria of requirements and elements of Reference Architectures have been rephrased in the format of a Self-Assessment questionnaire, with a seven-criterion scoring system, as explained in this document.

In this format, even with limited background knowledge of Reference Architectures, a manager can quickly review existing operations to determine how they measure up to the standards. This in turn can serve as the starting point of a 'gap analysis' to identify management tools or system elements that might usefully be implemented in the organization to help improve overall performance.

How to use the Self-Assessment

On the following pages are a series of questions to identify to what extent your Reference Architectures initiative is complete in comparison to the requirements set in standards.

To facilitate answering the questions, there is a space in front of each question to enter a score on a scale of '1' to '5'.

1 Strongly Disagree

2 Disagree

3 Neutral

4 Agree

5 Strongly Agree

Read the question and rate it with the following in front of mind:

'In my belief, the answer to this question is clearly defined'.

There are two ways in which you can choose to interpret this statement;
1. how aware are you that the answer to the question is clearly defined
2. for more in-depth analysis you can choose to gather evidence and confirm the answer to the question. This obviously will take more time, most Self-Assessment users opt for the first way to interpret the question and dig deeper later on based on the outcome of the overall Self-Assessment.

A score of '1' would mean that the answer is not clear at all, where a '5' would mean the answer is crystal clear and defined. Leave emtpy when the question is not applicable or you don't want to answer it, you can skip it without affecting your score. Write your score in the space provided.

After you have responded to all the appropriate statements in each section, compute your average score for that section, using the formula provided, and round to the nearest tenth. Then transfer to the corresponding spoke in the Reference Architectures Scorecard on the second next page of the Self-Assessment.

Your completed Reference Architectures Scorecard will give you a clear presentation of which Reference Architectures areas need attention.

Reference Architectures Scorecard Example

Example of how the finalized Scorecard can look like:

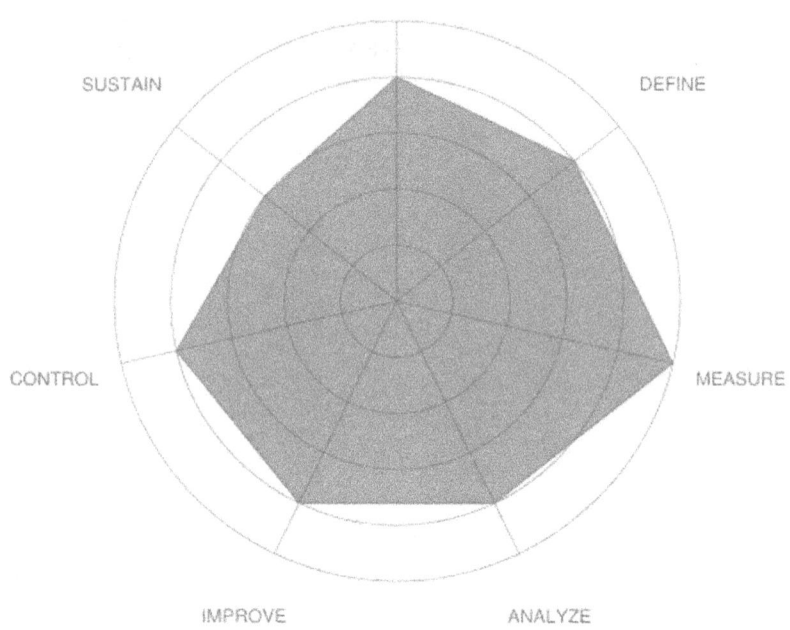

Reference Architectures Scorecard

Your Scores:

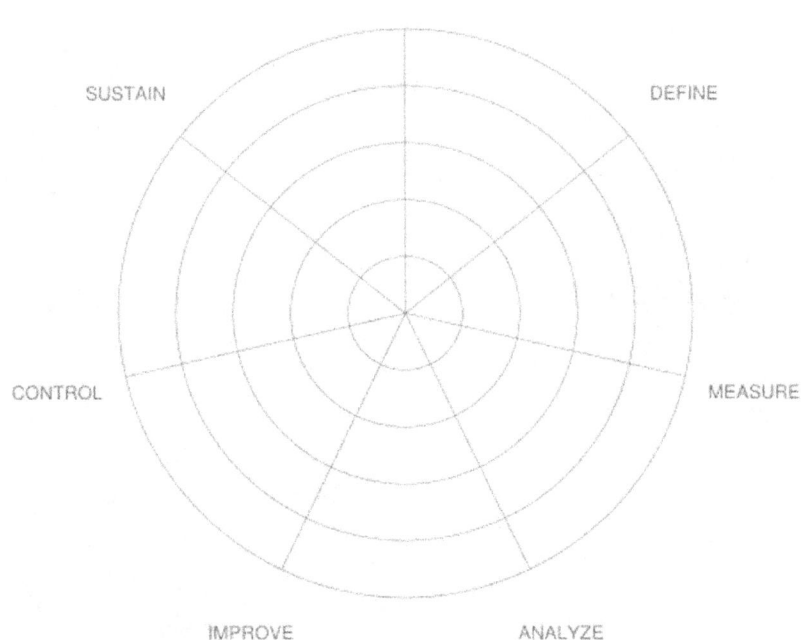

BEGINNING OF THE SELF-ASSESSMENT:

CRITERION #1: RECOGNIZE

INTENT: Be aware of the need for change. Recognize that there is an unfavorable variation, problem or symptom.

In my belief, the answer to this question is clearly defined:

5 Strongly Agree

4 Agree

3 Neutral

2 Disagree

1 Strongly Disagree

1. Can management personnel recognize the monetary benefit of Reference Architectures?
<--- Score

2. How do you assess your Reference Architectures workforce capability and capacity needs, including skills, competencies, and staffing levels?
<--- Score

3. How does it fit into your organizational needs and tasks?
<--- Score

4. What tools and technologies are needed for a custom Reference Architectures project?
<--- Score

5. Will a response program recognize when a crisis occurs and provide some level of response?
<--- Score

6. Who needs budgets?
<--- Score

7. How are you going to measure success?
<--- Score

8. Are controls defined to recognize and contain problems?
<--- Score

9. What activities does the governance board need to consider?
<--- Score

10. Is the need for organizational change recognized?
<--- Score

11. Who defines the rules in relation to any given issue?
<--- Score

12. Do you have/need 24-hour access to key personnel?
<--- Score

13. Who are your key stakeholders who need to sign off?
<--- Score

14. What resources or support might you need?
<--- Score

15. How do you identify subcontractor relationships?
<--- Score

16. Do you recognize Reference Architectures achievements?
<--- Score

17. What needs to stay?
<--- Score

18. What are the Reference Architectures resources needed?
<--- Score

19. How do you identify the kinds of information that you will need?
<--- Score

20. For your Reference Architectures project, identify and describe the business environment, is there more than one layer to the business environment?
<--- Score

21. Where is training needed?
<--- Score

22. Why is this needed?
<--- Score

23. What problems are you facing and how do you consider Reference Architectures will circumvent those obstacles?
<--- Score

24. What is the problem and/or vulnerability?
<--- Score

25. Who needs what information?
<--- Score

26. Which needs are not included or involved?
<--- Score

27. Consider your own Reference Architectures project, what types of organizational problems do you think might be causing or affecting your problem, based on the work done so far?
<--- Score

28. What training and capacity building actions are needed to implement proposed reforms?
<--- Score

29. Are your goals realistic? Do you need to redefine your problem? Perhaps the problem has changed or maybe you have reached your goal and need to set a new one?
<--- Score

30. What creative shifts do you need to take?
<--- Score

31. What are the minority interests and what amount of minority interests can be recognized?

<--- Score

32. Are there regulatory / compliance issues?
<--- Score

33. What do employees need in the short term?
<--- Score

34. What is the extent or complexity of the Reference Architectures problem?
<--- Score

35. What vendors make products that address the Reference Architectures needs?
<--- Score

36. Will Reference Architectures deliverables need to be tested and, if so, by whom?
<--- Score

37. Which information does the Reference Architectures business case need to include?
<--- Score

38. Are you dealing with any of the same issues today as yesterday? What can you do about this?
<--- Score

39. Where do you need to exercise leadership?
<--- Score

40. Are problem definition and motivation clearly presented?
<--- Score

41. Are employees recognized for desired behaviors?

<--- Score

42. What should be considered when identifying available resources, constraints, and deadlines?
<--- Score

43. As a sponsor, customer or management, how important is it to meet goals, objectives?
<--- Score

44. What are the timeframes required to resolve each of the issues/problems?
<--- Score

45. What situation(s) led to this Reference Architectures Self Assessment?
<--- Score

46. Will new equipment/products be required to facilitate Reference Architectures delivery, for example is new software needed?
<--- Score

47. Have you identified your Reference Architectures key performance indicators?
<--- Score

48. Who else hopes to benefit from it?
<--- Score

49. Who should resolve the Reference Architectures issues?
<--- Score

50. What are your needs in relation to Reference Architectures skills, labor, equipment, and markets?

<--- Score

51. Is it needed?
<--- Score

52. Does the problem have ethical dimensions?
<--- Score

53. What prevents you from making the changes you know will make you a more effective Reference Architectures leader?
<--- Score

54. What do you need to start doing?
<--- Score

55. What needs to be done?
<--- Score

56. Who needs to know?
<--- Score

57. What are the expected benefits of Reference Architectures to the stakeholder?
<--- Score

58. Are losses recognized in a timely manner?
<--- Score

59. Did you miss any major Reference Architectures issues?
<--- Score

60. Does Reference Architectures create potential expectations in other areas that need to be recognized and considered?

<--- Score

61. What would happen if Reference Architectures weren't done?
<--- Score

62. Would you recognize a threat from the inside?
<--- Score

63. What is the Reference Architectures problem definition? What do you need to resolve?
<--- Score

64. To what extent would your organization benefit from being recognized as a award recipient?
<--- Score

65. Whom do you really need or want to serve?
<--- Score

66. What extra resources will you need?
<--- Score

67. How do you recognize an objection?
<--- Score

68. Are there recognized Reference Architectures problems?
<--- Score

69. Is the quality assurance team identified?
<--- Score

70. Are there any specific expectations or concerns about the Reference Architectures team, Reference Architectures itself?

<--- Score

71. What Reference Architectures coordination do you need?
<--- Score

72. How do you take a forward-looking perspective in identifying Reference Architectures research related to market response and models?
<--- Score

73. How are training requirements identified?
<--- Score

74. What does Reference Architectures success mean to the stakeholders?
<--- Score

75. Who needs to know about Reference Architectures?
<--- Score

76. Which issues are too important to ignore?
<--- Score

77. What is the recognized need?
<--- Score

78. Is it clear when you think of the day ahead of you what activities and tasks you need to complete?
<--- Score

79. Think about the people you identified for your Reference Architectures project and the project responsibilities you would assign to them, what kind of training do you think they would need to perform

these responsibilities effectively?
<--- Score

80. Why the need?
<--- Score

81. What is the smallest subset of the problem you can usefully solve?
<--- Score

82. How much are sponsors, customers, partners, stakeholders involved in Reference Architectures? In other words, what are the risks, if Reference Architectures does not deliver successfully?
<--- Score

83. What Reference Architectures events should you attend?
<--- Score

84. Are there any revenue recognition issues?
<--- Score

85. What Reference Architectures problem should be solved?
<--- Score

86. What are the clients issues and concerns?
<--- Score

87. Does your organization need more Reference Architectures education?
<--- Score

88. What Reference Architectures capabilities do you need?

<--- Score

89. How do you recognize an Reference Architectures objection?
<--- Score

90. How are the Reference Architectures's objectives aligned to the group's overall stakeholder strategy?
<--- Score

91. How can auditing be a preventative security measure?
<--- Score

92. What else needs to be measured?
<--- Score

93. What is the problem or issue?
<--- Score

94. Will it solve real problems?
<--- Score

95. What are the stakeholder objectives to be achieved with Reference Architectures?
<--- Score

96. Do you need to avoid or amend any Reference Architectures activities?
<--- Score

Add up total points for this section:
_ _ _ _ _ = Total points for this section

Divided by: _ _ _ _ _ _ (number of statements answered) = _ _ _ _ _ _

Average score for this section

Transfer your score to the Reference
Architectures Index at the beginning of
the Self-Assessment.

CRITERION #2: DEFINE:

INTENT: Formulate the stakeholder problem. Define the problem, needs and objectives.

In my belief, the answer to this question is clearly defined:

5 Strongly Agree

4 Agree

3 Neutral

2 Disagree

1 Strongly Disagree

1. Are task requirements clearly defined?
<--- Score

2. What customer feedback methods were used to solicit their input?
<--- Score

3. When are meeting minutes sent out? Who is on the distribution list?

<--- Score

4. What is the context?
<--- Score

5. Is the team equipped with available and reliable resources?
<--- Score

6. What key stakeholder process output measure(s) does Reference Architectures leverage and how?
<--- Score

7. Who is gathering Reference Architectures information?
<--- Score

8. Has anyone else (internal or external to the group) attempted to solve this problem or a similar one before? If so, what knowledge can be leveraged from these previous efforts?
<--- Score

9. What are the dynamics of the communication plan?
<--- Score

10. How do you manage scope?
<--- Score

11. How have you defined all Reference Architectures requirements first?
<--- Score

12. How and when will the baselines be defined?
<--- Score

13. What scope to assess?
<--- Score

14. How did the Reference Architectures manager receive input to the development of a Reference Architectures improvement plan and the estimated completion dates/times of each activity?
<--- Score

15. Who approved the Reference Architectures scope?
<--- Score

16. Will team members regularly document their Reference Architectures work?
<--- Score

17. Does the scope remain the same?
<--- Score

18. How do you gather Reference Architectures requirements?
<--- Score

19. What are the requirements for audit information?
<--- Score

20. What are the record-keeping requirements of Reference Architectures activities?
<--- Score

21. Are accountability and ownership for Reference Architectures clearly defined?
<--- Score

22. Has a team charter been developed and communicated?

<--- Score

23. Have the customer needs been translated into specific, measurable requirements? How?
<--- Score

24. How is the team tracking and documenting its work?
<--- Score

25. What is the scope?
<--- Score

26. Are there different segments of customers?
<--- Score

27. Is scope creep really all bad news?
<--- Score

28. Have specific policy objectives been defined?
<--- Score

29. What are the Reference Architectures use cases?
<--- Score

30. Does the team have regular meetings?
<--- Score

31. Is it clearly defined in and to your organization what you do?
<--- Score

32. What intelligence can you gather?
<--- Score

33. Are roles and responsibilities formally defined?

<--- Score

34. How can the value of Reference Architectures be defined?
<--- Score

35. Is the improvement team aware of the different versions of a process: what they think it is vs. what it actually is vs. what it should be vs. what it could be?
<--- Score

36. How do you build the right business case?
<--- Score

37. If substitutes have been appointed, have they been briefed on the Reference Architectures goals and received regular communications as to the progress to date?
<--- Score

38. Are approval levels defined for contracts and supplements to contracts?
<--- Score

39. Is the team adequately staffed with the desired cross-functionality? If not, what additional resources are available to the team?
<--- Score

40. Is special Reference Architectures user knowledge required?
<--- Score

41. What is the scope of the Reference Architectures effort?
<--- Score

42. What are the core elements of the Reference Architectures business case?
<--- Score

43. How was the 'as is' process map developed, reviewed, verified and validated?
<--- Score

44. Is the work to date meeting requirements?
<--- Score

45. What are the compelling stakeholder reasons for embarking on Reference Architectures?
<--- Score

46. Are different versions of process maps needed to account for the different types of inputs?
<--- Score

47. Has the direction changed at all during the course of Reference Architectures? If so, when did it change and why?
<--- Score

48. What are the rough order estimates on cost savings/opportunities that Reference Architectures brings?
<--- Score

49. What critical content must be communicated – who, what, when, where, and how?
<--- Score

50. Are audit criteria, scope, frequency and methods defined?

<--- Score

51. Are the Reference Architectures requirements testable?
<--- Score

52. What Reference Architectures requirements should be gathered?
<--- Score

53. Are there any constraints known that bear on the ability to perform Reference Architectures work? How is the team addressing them?
<--- Score

54. What sort of initial information to gather?
<--- Score

55. Has a project plan, Gantt chart, or similar been developed/completed?
<--- Score

56. Is there a clear Reference Architectures case definition?
<--- Score

57. What are the Roles and Responsibilities for each team member and its leadership? Where is this documented?
<--- Score

58. Has the improvement team collected the 'voice of the customer' (obtained feedback – qualitative and quantitative)?
<--- Score

59. How would you define the culture at your organization, how susceptible is it to Reference Architectures changes?
<--- Score

60. Will team members perform Reference Architectures work when assigned and in a timely fashion?
<--- Score

61. What information do you gather?
<--- Score

62. How do you keep key subject matter experts in the loop?
<--- Score

63. Is there any additional Reference Architectures definition of success?
<--- Score

64. Has a high-level 'as is' process map been completed, verified and validated?
<--- Score

65. How does the Reference Architectures manager ensure against scope creep?
<--- Score

66. What are the boundaries of the scope? What is in bounds and what is not? What is the start point? What is the stop point?
<--- Score

67. Is Reference Architectures required?
<--- Score

68. How often are the team meetings?
<--- Score

69. What scope do you want your strategy to cover?
<--- Score

70. Who defines (or who defined) the rules and roles?
<--- Score

71. Has/have the customer(s) been identified?
<--- Score

72. What system do you use for gathering Reference Architectures information?
<--- Score

73. Are the Reference Architectures requirements complete?
<--- Score

74. Is there regularly 100% attendance at the team meetings? If not, have appointed substitutes attended to preserve cross-functionality and full representation?
<--- Score

75. What sources do you use to gather information for a Reference Architectures study?
<--- Score

76. What gets examined?
<--- Score

77. What baselines are required to be defined and managed?

<--- Score

78. What happens if Reference Architectures's scope changes?
<--- Score

79. What is the definition of Reference Architectures excellence?
<--- Score

80. Have all of the relationships been defined properly?
<--- Score

81. How do you manage unclear Reference Architectures requirements?
<--- Score

82. What is the definition of success?
<--- Score

83. What Reference Architectures services do you require?
<--- Score

84. How do you manage changes in Reference Architectures requirements?
<--- Score

85. How would you define Reference Architectures leadership?
<--- Score

86. Is there a Reference Architectures management charter, including stakeholder case, problem and goal statements, scope, milestones, roles and

responsibilities, communication plan?
<--- Score

87. Is there a completed, verified, and validated high-level 'as is' (not 'should be' or 'could be') stakeholder process map?
<--- Score

88. Is data collected and displayed to better understand customer(s) critical needs and requirements.
<--- Score

89. Are all requirements met?
<--- Score

90. Is the scope of Reference Architectures defined?
<--- Score

91. What knowledge or experience is required?
<--- Score

92. Is the current 'as is' process being followed? If not, what are the discrepancies?
<--- Score

93. How do you gather the stories?
<--- Score

94. Who are the Reference Architectures improvement team members, including Management Leads and Coaches?
<--- Score

95. Is there a critical path to deliver Reference Architectures results?

<--- Score

96. Who is gathering information?
<--- Score

97. What is in scope?
<--- Score

98. What is the scope of the Reference Architectures work?
<--- Score

99. In what way can you redefine the criteria of choice clients have in your category in your favor?
<--- Score

100. How will variation in the actual durations of each activity be dealt with to ensure that the expected Reference Architectures results are met?
<--- Score

101. What would be the goal or target for a Reference Architectures's improvement team?
<--- Score

102. Are customer(s) identified and segmented according to their different needs and requirements?
<--- Score

103. Scope of sensitive information?
<--- Score

104. What are the Reference Architectures tasks and definitions?
<--- Score

105. What specifically is the problem? Where does it occur? When does it occur? What is its extent?
<--- Score

106. Is Reference Architectures currently on schedule according to the plan?
<--- Score

107. How do you gather requirements?
<--- Score

108. Has the Reference Architectures work been fairly and/or equitably divided and delegated among team members who are qualified and capable to perform the work? Has everyone contributed?
<--- Score

109. Where can you gather more information?
<--- Score

110. What is out of scope?
<--- Score

111. What is the scope of Reference Architectures?
<--- Score

112. What constraints exist that might impact the team?
<--- Score

113. Is the Reference Architectures scope complete and appropriately sized?
<--- Score

114. How do you catch Reference Architectures definition inconsistencies?

<--- Score

115. How will the Reference Architectures team and the group measure complete success of Reference Architectures?
<--- Score

116. What information should you gather?
<--- Score

117. Is the Reference Architectures scope manageable?
<--- Score

118. How are consistent Reference Architectures definitions important?
<--- Score

119. What was the context?
<--- Score

120. What is the worst case scenario?
<--- Score

121. Do you have a Reference Architectures success story or case study ready to tell and share?
<--- Score

122. When is/was the Reference Architectures start date?
<--- Score

123. What is a worst-case scenario for losses?
<--- Score

124. Has everyone on the team, including the team

leaders, been properly trained?
<--- Score

125. Do you all define Reference Architectures in the same way?
<--- Score

126. Do the problem and goal statements meet the SMART criteria (specific, measurable, attainable, relevant, and time-bound)?
<--- Score

127. Is Reference Architectures linked to key stakeholder goals and objectives?
<--- Score

128. Have all basic functions of Reference Architectures been defined?
<--- Score

129. The political context: who holds power?
<--- Score

130. Is there a completed SIPOC representation, describing the Suppliers, Inputs, Process, Outputs, and Customers?
<--- Score

131. When is the estimated completion date?
<--- Score

132. Has a Reference Architectures requirement not been met?
<--- Score

133. What is out-of-scope initially?

<--- Score

134. Has your scope been defined?
<--- Score

135. How do you hand over Reference Architectures context?
<--- Score

136. What are the tasks and definitions?
<--- Score

137. Will a Reference Architectures production readiness review be required?
<--- Score

Add up total points for this section:
_ _ _ _ _ = Total points for this section

Divided by: _ _ _ _ _ _ (number of statements answered) = _ _ _ _ _ _
Average score for this section

Transfer your score to the Reference Architectures Index at the beginning of the Self-Assessment.

CRITERION #3: MEASURE:

INTENT: Gather the correct data. Measure the current performance and evolution of the situation.

In my belief, the answer to this question is clearly defined:

5 Strongly Agree

4 Agree

3 Neutral

2 Disagree

1 Strongly Disagree

1. What do people want to verify?
<--- Score

2. What are the Reference Architectures key cost drivers?
<--- Score

3. Have design-to-cost goals been established?
<--- Score

4. Have you included everything in your Reference Architectures cost models?
<--- Score

5. Does the Reference Architectures task fit the client's priorities?
<--- Score

6. When a disaster occurs, who gets priority?
<--- Score

7. What is the total cost related to deploying Reference Architectures, including any consulting or professional services?
<--- Score

8. How frequently do you track Reference Architectures measures?
<--- Score

9. What does losing customers cost your organization?
<--- Score

10. What is your Reference Architectures quality cost segregation study?
<--- Score

11. Are actual costs in line with budgeted costs?
<--- Score

12. How do you verify your resources?
<--- Score

13. How are costs allocated?
<--- Score

14. What tests verify requirements?
<--- Score

15. What is an unallowable cost?
<--- Score

16. How do you verify the Reference Architectures requirements quality?
<--- Score

17. What measurements are being captured?
<--- Score

18. Where can you go to verify the info?
<--- Score

19. What are the current costs of the Reference Architectures process?
<--- Score

20. What can be used to verify compliance?
<--- Score

21. Are supply costs steady or fluctuating?
<--- Score

22. How much does it cost?
<--- Score

23. Is the solution cost-effective?
<--- Score

24. When are costs are incurred?
<--- Score

25. When should you bother with diagrams?
<--- Score

26. How will effects be measured?
<--- Score

27. What are the estimated costs of proposed changes?
<--- Score

28. How do you verify and validate the Reference Architectures data?
<--- Score

29. Does management have the right priorities among projects?
<--- Score

30. What are the costs of delaying Reference Architectures action?
<--- Score

31. How can you reduce the costs of obtaining inputs?
<--- Score

32. How do you verify the authenticity of the data and information used?
<--- Score

33. What causes extra work or rework?
<--- Score

34. How can you measure the performance?
<--- Score

35. Is there an opportunity to verify requirements?

<--- Score

36. Did you tackle the cause or the symptom?
<--- Score

37. What are you verifying?
<--- Score

38. Why do you expend time and effort to implement measurement, for whom?
<--- Score

39. How do you measure efficient delivery of Reference Architectures services?
<--- Score

40. How do you verify and develop ideas and innovations?
<--- Score

41. Why do the measurements/indicators matter?
<--- Score

42. What are hidden Reference Architectures quality costs?
<--- Score

43. Are missed Reference Architectures opportunities costing your organization money?
<--- Score

44. How is progress measured?
<--- Score

45. What causes innovation to fail or succeed in your organization?

<--- Score

46. Are the measurements objective?
<--- Score

47. How will success or failure be measured?
<--- Score

48. Do you have a flow diagram of what happens?
<--- Score

49. Which Reference Architectures impacts are
significant?
<--- Score

50. What are the costs?
<--- Score

51. What is the cause of any Reference Architectures
gaps?
<--- Score

52. Are there measurements based on task
performance?
<--- Score

53. How do you measure success?
<--- Score

54. Will Reference Architectures have an impact
on current business continuity, disaster recovery
processes and/or infrastructure?
<--- Score

55. What are your operating costs?
<--- Score

56. What relevant entities could be measured?
<--- Score

57. How do you control the overall costs of your work processes?
<--- Score

58. What methods are feasible and acceptable to estimate the impact of reforms?
<--- Score

59. What are the types and number of measures to use?
<--- Score

60. How do you verify performance?
<--- Score

61. Do you aggressively reward and promote the people who have the biggest impact on creating excellent Reference Architectures services/products?
<--- Score

62. Where is the cost?
<--- Score

63. How is the value delivered by Reference Architectures being measured?
<--- Score

64. How are measurements made?
<--- Score

65. What measurements are possible, practicable and meaningful?

<--- Score

66. How will you measure success?
<--- Score

67. Which costs should be taken into account?
<--- Score

68. Are there any easy-to-implement alternatives to Reference Architectures? Sometimes other solutions are available that do not require the cost implications of a full-blown project?
<--- Score

69. Are you aware of what could cause a problem?
<--- Score

70. How do you verify if Reference Architectures is built right?
<--- Score

71. What does your operating model cost?
<--- Score

72. Are you able to realize any cost savings?
<--- Score

73. Where is it measured?
<--- Score

74. Do you have an issue in getting priority?
<--- Score

75. Do you verify that corrective actions were taken?
<--- Score

76. What are the uncertainties surrounding estimates of impact?
<--- Score

77. How do you measure lifecycle phases?
<--- Score

78. What is your decision requirements diagram?
<--- Score

79. Is it possible to estimate the impact of unanticipated complexity such as wrong or failed assumptions, feedback, etcetera on proposed reforms?
<--- Score

80. What disadvantage does this cause for the user?
<--- Score

81. Was a business case (cost/benefit) developed?
<--- Score

82. How can you manage cost down?
<--- Score

83. Who should receive measurement reports?
<--- Score

84. How to cause the change?
<--- Score

85. Are Reference Architectures vulnerabilities categorized and prioritized?
<--- Score

86. How do you measure variability?

<--- Score

87. Does a Reference Architectures quantification method exist?
<--- Score

88. Are there competing Reference Architectures priorities?
<--- Score

89. What users will be impacted?
<--- Score

90. What are your customers expectations and measures?
<--- Score

91. What details are required of the Reference Architectures cost structure?
<--- Score

92. Are the units of measure consistent?
<--- Score

93. What are the Reference Architectures investment costs?
<--- Score

94. What drives O&M cost?
<--- Score

95. What are allowable costs?
<--- Score

96. What evidence is there and what is measured?
<--- Score

97. How will measures be used to manage and adapt?
<--- Score

98. What potential environmental factors impact the Reference Architectures effort?
<--- Score

99. Are the Reference Architectures benefits worth its costs?
<--- Score

100. How do your measurements capture actionable Reference Architectures information for use in exceeding your customers expectations and securing your customers engagement?
<--- Score

101. What causes mismanagement?
<--- Score

102. How can you measure Reference Architectures in a systematic way?
<--- Score

103. How will costs be allocated?
<--- Score

104. What are the operational costs after Reference Architectures deployment?
<--- Score

105. How long to keep data and how to manage retention costs?
<--- Score

106. What are your key Reference Architectures organizational performance measures, including key short and longer-term financial measures?
<--- Score

107. Do you effectively measure and reward individual and team performance?
<--- Score

108. How is performance measured?
<--- Score

109. What are your primary costs, revenues, assets?
<--- Score

110. What would be a real cause for concern?
<--- Score

111. Has a cost center been established?
<--- Score

112. What causes investor action?
<--- Score

113. What is the root cause(s) of the problem?
<--- Score

114. What harm might be caused?
<--- Score

115. Among the Reference Architectures product and service cost to be estimated, which is considered hardest to estimate?
<--- Score

116. At what cost?

<--- Score

117. How will you measure your Reference
Architectures effectiveness?
<--- Score

118. How can you reduce costs?
<--- Score

119. What could cause delays in the schedule?
<--- Score

120. Are indirect costs charged to the Reference
Architectures program?
<--- Score

121. How can a Reference Architectures test verify
your ideas or assumptions?
<--- Score

122. Is the cost worth the Reference Architectures
effort ?
<--- Score

123. What is the cost of rework?
<--- Score

124. What is the Reference Architectures business
impact?
<--- Score

125. What are the costs and benefits?
<--- Score

126. Who pays the cost?
<--- Score

127. How do you quantify and qualify impacts?
<--- Score

128. What does a Test Case verify?
<--- Score

129. What do you measure and why?
<--- Score

130. How sensitive must the Reference Architectures strategy be to cost?
<--- Score

131. How will your organization measure success?
<--- Score

132. Have you made assumptions about the shape of the future, particularly its impact on your customers and competitors?
<--- Score

133. Do the benefits outweigh the costs?
<--- Score

134. Do you have any cost Reference Architectures limitation requirements?
<--- Score

135. What is the total fixed cost?
<--- Score

136. How do you prevent mis-estimating cost?
<--- Score

137. What would it cost to replace your technology?

<--- Score

138. What happens if cost savings do not materialize?
<--- Score

139. What could cause you to change course?
<--- Score

Add up total points for this section:
_____ = Total points for this section

Divided by: _____ (number of
statements answered) = _____
Average score for this section

Transfer your score to the Reference
Architectures Index at the beginning of
the Self-Assessment.

CRITERION #4: ANALYZE:

INTENT: Analyze causes, assumptions and hypotheses.

In my belief, the answer to this question is clearly defined:

5 Strongly Agree

4 Agree

3 Neutral

2 Disagree

1 Strongly Disagree

1. Do your leaders quickly bounce back from setbacks?
<--- Score

2. What process should you select for improvement?
<--- Score

3. What methods do you use to gather Reference Architectures data?
<--- Score

4. What systems/processes must you excel at?
<--- Score

5. Were there any improvement opportunities identified from the process analysis?
<--- Score

6. How is the Reference Architectures Value Stream Mapping managed?
<--- Score

7. What information qualified as important?
<--- Score

8. What is the oversight process?
<--- Score

9. What data is gathered?
<--- Score

10. Is the required Reference Architectures data gathered?
<--- Score

11. An organizationally feasible system request is one that considers the mission, goals and objectives of the organization, key questions are: is the Reference Architectures solution request practical and will it solve a problem or take advantage of an opportunity to achieve company goals?
<--- Score

12. How are outputs preserved and protected?
<--- Score

13. What qualifications do Reference Architectures leaders need?
<--- Score

14. What are your current levels and trends in key Reference Architectures measures or indicators of product and process performance that are important to and directly serve your customers?
<--- Score

15. How will the change process be managed?
<--- Score

16. What is your organizations process which leads to recognition of value generation?
<--- Score

17. Who will gather what data?
<--- Score

18. What successful thing are you doing today that may be blinding you to new growth opportunities?
<--- Score

19. What quality tools were used to get through the analyze phase?
<--- Score

20. Was a cause-and-effect diagram used to explore the different types of causes (or sources of variation)?
<--- Score

21. What Reference Architectures metrics are outputs of the process?
<--- Score

22. What Reference Architectures data should be managed?
<--- Score

23. How many input/output points does it require?
<--- Score

24. What are the disruptive Reference Architectures technologies that enable your organization to radically change your business processes?
<--- Score

25. What controls do you have in place to protect data?
<--- Score

26. How has the Reference Architectures data been gathered?
<--- Score

27. What, related to, Reference Architectures processes does your organization outsource?
<--- Score

28. How does the organization define, manage, and improve its Reference Architectures processes?
<--- Score

29. What are the personnel training and qualifications required?
<--- Score

30. How do you define collaboration and team output?
<--- Score

31. What qualifies as competition?
<--- Score

32. What does the data say about the performance of the stakeholder process?
<--- Score

33. Think about the functions involved in your Reference Architectures project, what processes flow from these functions?
<--- Score

34. How will the data be checked for quality?
<--- Score

35. What is your organizations system for selecting qualified vendors?
<--- Score

36. How much data can be collected in the given timeframe?
<--- Score

37. Are you missing Reference Architectures opportunities?
<--- Score

38. What resources go in to get the desired output?
<--- Score

39. What conclusions were drawn from the team's data collection and analysis? How did the team reach these conclusions?
<--- Score

40. Who owns what data?

<--- Score

41. Do your employees have the opportunity to do what they do best everyday?
<--- Score

42. What is the output?
<--- Score

43. Do your contracts/agreements contain data security obligations?
<--- Score

44. What training and qualifications will you need?
<--- Score

45. What are your outputs?
<--- Score

46. Was a detailed process map created to amplify critical steps of the 'as is' stakeholder process?
<--- Score

47. Who qualifies to gain access to data?
<--- Score

48. Do you, as a leader, bounce back quickly from setbacks?
<--- Score

49. How is the way you as the leader think and process information affecting your organizational culture?
<--- Score

50. What are your Reference Architectures processes?
<--- Score

51. What are the best opportunities for value improvement?
<--- Score

52. Are all team members qualified for all tasks?
<--- Score

53. How do you use Reference Architectures data and information to support organizational decision making and innovation?
<--- Score

54. Is there any way to speed up the process?
<--- Score

55. How do mission and objectives affect the Reference Architectures processes of your organization?
<--- Score

56. What will drive Reference Architectures change?
<--- Score

57. Is the final output clearly identified?
<--- Score

58. A compounding model resolution with available relevant data can often provide insight towards a solution methodology; which Reference Architectures models, tools and techniques are necessary?
<--- Score

59. What Reference Architectures data do you gather or use now?
<--- Score

60. What qualifications are needed?
<--- Score

61. How will the Reference Architectures data be captured?
<--- Score

62. What other organizational variables, such as reward systems or communication systems, affect the performance of this Reference Architectures process?
<--- Score

63. Were Pareto charts (or similar) used to portray the 'heavy hitters' (or key sources of variation)?
<--- Score

64. Have you defined which data is gathered how?
<--- Score

65. What are your key performance measures or indicators and in-process measures for the control and improvement of your Reference Architectures processes?
<--- Score

66. How often will data be collected for measures?
<--- Score

67. Are all staff in core Reference Architectures subjects Highly Qualified?
<--- Score

68. Should you invest in industry-recognized qualifications?
<--- Score

69. Record-keeping requirements flow from the records needed as inputs, outputs, controls and for transformation of a Reference Architectures process, are the records needed as inputs to the Reference Architectures process available?
<--- Score

70. How is the data gathered?
<--- Score

71. What process improvements will be needed?
<--- Score

72. Do you have the authority to produce the output?
<--- Score

73. What are the revised rough estimates of the financial savings/opportunity for Reference Architectures improvements?
<--- Score

74. How are the new Big Data developments captured in new Reference Architectures?
<--- Score

75. What are the necessary qualifications?
<--- Score

76. What did the team gain from developing a sub-process map?
<--- Score

77. What Reference Architectures data will be collected?
<--- Score

78. What kind of crime could a potential new hire have committed that would not only not disqualify him/her from being hired by your organization, but would actually indicate that he/she might be a particularly good fit?
<--- Score

79. Who is involved in the management review process?
<--- Score

80. What output to create?
<--- Score

81. Think about some of the processes you undertake within your organization, which do you own?
<--- Score

82. Is pre-qualification of suppliers carried out?
<--- Score

83. What qualifications are necessary?
<--- Score

84. What tools were used to narrow the list of possible causes?
<--- Score

85. Are Reference Architectures changes recognized early enough to be approved through the regular process?
<--- Score

86. What types of data do your Reference Architectures indicators require?

<--- Score

87. Where is the data coming from to measure compliance?
<--- Score

88. Where can you get qualified talent today?
<--- Score

89. Identify an operational issue in your organization, for example, could a particular task be done more quickly or more efficiently by Reference Architectures?
<--- Score

90. How will corresponding data be collected?
<--- Score

91. What is the Value Stream Mapping?
<--- Score

92. Do you understand your management processes today?
<--- Score

93. What are your current levels and trends in key measures or indicators of Reference Architectures product and process performance that are important to and directly serve your customers? How do these results compare with the performance of your competitors and other organizations with similar offerings?
<--- Score

94. What are the processes for audit reporting and management?
<--- Score

95. What internal processes need improvement?
<--- Score

96. Where is Reference Architectures data gathered?
<--- Score

97. Who is involved with workflow mapping?
<--- Score

98. What Reference Architectures data should be collected?
<--- Score

99. How do you identify specific Reference Architectures investment opportunities and emerging trends?
<--- Score

100. When should a process be art not science?
<--- Score

101. What qualifications and skills do you need?
<--- Score

102. Do staff qualifications match your project?
<--- Score

103. How is Reference Architectures data gathered?
<--- Score

104. What is the Reference Architectures Driver?
<--- Score

105. What is the complexity of the output produced?
<--- Score

106. What other jobs or tasks affect the performance of the steps in the Reference Architectures process?
<--- Score

107. Who gets your output?
<--- Score

108. How do you ensure that the Reference Architectures opportunity is realistic?
<--- Score

109. Were any designed experiments used to generate additional insight into the data analysis?
<--- Score

110. How do you measure the operational performance of your key work systems and processes, including productivity, cycle time, and other appropriate measures of process effectiveness, efficiency, and innovation?
<--- Score

111. Is the suppliers process defined and controlled?
<--- Score

112. How is data used for program management and improvement?
<--- Score

113. What are your best practices for minimizing Reference Architectures project risk, while demonstrating incremental value and quick wins throughout the Reference Architectures project lifecycle?
<--- Score

114. What data do you need to collect?
<--- Score

115. What tools were used to generate the list of possible causes?
<--- Score

116. Has an output goal been set?
<--- Score

117. Do quality systems drive continuous improvement?
<--- Score

118. Are your outputs consistent?
<--- Score

119. What do you need to qualify?
<--- Score

120. Can you add value to the current Reference Architectures decision-making process (largely qualitative) by incorporating uncertainty modeling (more quantitative)?
<--- Score

121. How are new Big Data developments captured in new Reference Architectures?
<--- Score

122. How difficult is it to qualify what Reference Architectures ROI is?
<--- Score

123. What are the Reference Architectures design

outputs?
<--- Score

124. Is the Reference Architectures process severely broken such that a re-design is necessary?
<--- Score

125. How do your work systems and key work processes relate to and capitalize on your core competencies?
<--- Score

126. What are evaluation criteria for the output?
<--- Score

127. Who will facilitate the team and process?
<--- Score

128. What were the financial benefits resulting from any 'ground fruit or low-hanging fruit' (quick fixes)?
<--- Score

129. What were the crucial 'moments of truth' on the process map?
<--- Score

130. What is the cost of poor quality as supported by the team's analysis?
<--- Score

131. Is there an established change management process?
<--- Score

Add up total points for this section:
_ _ _ _ _ = Total points for this section

Divided by: _____ (number of
statements answered) = _____
Average score for this section

Transfer your score to the Reference
Architectures Index at the beginning of
the Self-Assessment.

CRITERION #5: IMPROVE:

INTENT: Develop a practical solution. Innovate, establish and test the solution and to measure the results.

In my belief, the answer to this question is clearly defined:

5 Strongly Agree

4 Agree

3 Neutral

2 Disagree

1 Strongly Disagree

1. What is the team's contingency plan for potential problems occurring in implementation?
<--- Score

2. What is Reference Architectures risk?
<--- Score

3. Why improve in the first place?
<--- Score

4. Have you achieved Reference Architectures improvements?
<--- Score

5. When you map the key players in your own work and the types/domains of relationships with them, which relationships do you find easy and which challenging, and why?
<--- Score

6. Are events managed to resolution?
<--- Score

7. Will the controls trigger any other risks?
<--- Score

8. What should a proof of concept or pilot accomplish?
<--- Score

9. If you could go back in time five years, what decision would you make differently? What is your best guess as to what decision you're making today you might regret five years from now?
<--- Score

10. How will you know that you have improved?
<--- Score

11. Where do the Reference Architectures decisions reside?
<--- Score

12. How risky is your organization?
<--- Score

13. Does the goal represent a desired result that can be measured?
<--- Score

14. What tools do you use once you have decided on a Reference Architectures strategy and more importantly how do you choose?
<--- Score

15. How do you keep improving Reference Architectures?
<--- Score

16. How significant is the improvement in the eyes of the end user?
<--- Score

17. Can you identify any significant risks or exposures to Reference Architectures third- parties (vendors, service providers, alliance partners etc) that concern you?
<--- Score

18. What are the expected Reference Architectures results?
<--- Score

19. Who controls the risk?
<--- Score

20. At what point will vulnerability assessments be performed once Reference Architectures is put into production (e.g., ongoing Risk Management after implementation)?
<--- Score

21. Is any Reference Architectures documentation required?

<--- Score

22. How do you deal with Reference Architectures risk?

<--- Score

23. Where do you need Reference Architectures improvement?

<--- Score

24. Is the Reference Architectures solution sustainable?

<--- Score

25. How do the Reference Architectures results compare with the performance of your competitors and other organizations with similar offerings?

<--- Score

26. How do you mitigate Reference Architectures risk?

<--- Score

27. Are decisions made in a timely manner?

<--- Score

28. What resources are required for the improvement efforts?

<--- Score

29. Who do you report Reference Architectures results to?

<--- Score

30. Who are the Reference Architectures decision-makers?
<--- Score

31. What criteria will you use to assess your Reference Architectures risks?
<--- Score

32. What Reference Architectures improvements can be made?
<--- Score

33. Are risk management tasks balanced centrally and locally?
<--- Score

34. What do you want to improve?
<--- Score

35. How can you improve performance?
<--- Score

36. Is there a high likelihood that any recommendations will achieve their intended results?
<--- Score

37. Is supporting Reference Architectures documentation required?
<--- Score

38. How will you know that a change is an improvement?
<--- Score

39. Do you cover the five essential competencies: Communication, Collaboration,Innovation,

Adaptability, and Leadership that improve an organizations ability to leverage the new Reference Architectures in a volatile global economy?
<--- Score

40. How do you measure risk?
<--- Score

41. How is knowledge sharing about risk management improved?
<--- Score

42. Who will be using the results of the measurement activities?
<--- Score

43. What improvements have been achieved?
<--- Score

44. What area needs the greatest improvement?
<--- Score

45. What practices helps your organization to develop its capacity to recognize patterns?
<--- Score

46. How will you recognize and celebrate results?
<--- Score

47. How can the phases of Reference Architectures development be identified?
<--- Score

48. How do you decide how much to remunerate an employee?
<--- Score

49. How do you improve your likelihood of success ?
<--- Score

50. What went well, what should change, what can improve?
<--- Score

51. What are your current levels and trends in key measures or indicators of workforce and leader development?
<--- Score

52. What needs improvement? Why?
<--- Score

53. How can you improve Reference Architectures?
<--- Score

54. Was a Reference Architectures charter developed?
<--- Score

55. Are the risks fully understood, reasonable and manageable?
<--- Score

56. Risk Identification: What are the possible risk events your organization faces in relation to Reference Architectures?
<--- Score

57. How do you manage and improve your Reference Architectures work systems to deliver customer value and achieve organizational success and sustainability?
<--- Score

58. How does the team improve its work?
<--- Score

59. How can you better manage risk?
<--- Score

60. What tools were used to tap into the creativity and encourage 'outside the box' thinking?
<--- Score

61. Are the key business and technology risks being managed?
<--- Score

62. What risks do you need to manage?
<--- Score

63. Are procedures documented for managing Reference Architectures risks?
<--- Score

64. Is risk periodically assessed?
<--- Score

65. Do the viable solutions scale to future needs?
<--- Score

66. Who makes the Reference Architectures decisions in your organization?
<--- Score

67. In the past few months, what is the smallest change you have made that has had the biggest positive result? What was it about that small change that produced the large return?
<--- Score

68. What are the implications of the one critical Reference Architectures decision 10 minutes, 10 months, and 10 years from now?
<--- Score

69. What are the affordable Reference Architectures risks?
<--- Score

70. What strategies for Reference Architectures improvement are successful?
<--- Score

71. For estimation problems, how do you develop an estimation statement?
<--- Score

72. What lessons, if any, from a pilot were incorporated into the design of the full-scale solution?
<--- Score

73. What were the underlying assumptions on the cost-benefit analysis?
<--- Score

74. Reference Architectures risk decisions: whose call Is It?
<--- Score

75. What is the Reference Architectures's sustainability risk?
<--- Score

76. Risk events: what are the things that could go wrong?

<--- Score

77. Who will be responsible for making the decisions to include or exclude requested changes once Reference Architectures is underway?
<--- Score

78. Do you combine technical expertise with business knowledge and Reference Architectures Key topics include lifecycles, development approaches, requirements and how to make a business case?
<--- Score

79. Who should make the Reference Architectures decisions?
<--- Score

80. Explorations of the frontiers of Reference Architectures will help you build influence, improve Reference Architectures, optimize decision making, and sustain change, what is your approach?
<--- Score

81. What tools were used to evaluate the potential solutions?
<--- Score

82. How do you improve productivity?
<--- Score

83. How will you measure the results?
<--- Score

84. Who manages supplier risk management in your organization?
<--- Score

85. Can the solution be designed and implemented within an acceptable time period?
<--- Score

86. Does a good decision guarantee a good outcome?
<--- Score

87. Do you need to do a usability evaluation?
<--- Score

88. How do you improve Reference Architectures service perception, and satisfaction?
<--- Score

89. Can you integrate quality management and risk management?
<--- Score

90. What is the risk?
<--- Score

91. How are Reference Architectures risks managed?
<--- Score

92. How do you measure improved Reference Architectures service perception, and satisfaction?
<--- Score

93. How do you define the solutions' scope?
<--- Score

94. Are you assessing Reference Architectures and risk?
<--- Score

95. Who are the key stakeholders for the Reference Architectures evaluation?
<--- Score

96. Who are the Reference Architectures decision makers?
<--- Score

97. What tools were most useful during the improve phase?
<--- Score

98. What are the concrete Reference Architectures results?
<--- Score

99. What actually has to improve and by how much?
<--- Score

100. Have you identified breakpoints and/or risk tolerances that will trigger broad consideration of a potential need for intervention or modification of strategy?
<--- Score

101. Are risk triggers captured?
<--- Score

102. Is the solution technically practical?
<--- Score

103. What are the Reference Architectures security risks?
<--- Score

104. How do you link measurement and risk?

<--- Score

105. Who are the people involved in developing and implementing Reference Architectures?
<--- Score

106. How do you manage Reference Architectures risk?
<--- Score

107. Do you have the optimal project management team structure?
<--- Score

108. How do you go about comparing Reference Architectures approaches/solutions?
<--- Score

109. What can you do to improve?
<--- Score

110. What assumptions are made about the solution and approach?
<--- Score

111. Are the most efficient solutions problem-specific?
<--- Score

112. How are policy decisions made and where?
<--- Score

113. How do you measure progress and evaluate training effectiveness?
<--- Score

114. What were the criteria for evaluating a Reference

Architectures pilot?
<--- Score

115. What current systems have to be understood and/or changed?
<--- Score

116. Is Reference Architectures documentation maintained?
<--- Score

117. Which Reference Architectures solution is appropriate?
<--- Score

118. How can skill-level changes improve Reference Architectures?
<--- Score

119. Who manages Reference Architectures risk?
<--- Score

120. Is the measure of success for Reference Architectures understandable to a variety of people?
<--- Score

121. Do vendor agreements bring new compliance risk ?
<--- Score

122. What alternative responses are available to manage risk?
<--- Score

123. What to do with the results or outcomes of measurements?

<--- Score

124. What is the magnitude of the improvements?
<--- Score

125. Is there any other Reference Architectures
solution?
<--- Score

126. How scalable is your Reference Architectures
solution?
<--- Score

127. How will you know when its improved?
<--- Score

128. How is continuous improvement applied to risk
management?
<--- Score

129. Is the Reference Architectures documentation
thorough?
<--- Score

130. Who will be responsible for documenting the
Reference Architectures requirements in detail?
<--- Score

131. Do those selected for the Reference Architectures
team have a good general understanding of what
Reference Architectures is all about?
<--- Score

   Add up total points for this section:
   _ _ _ _ _   = Total points for this section

Divided by: _____ (number of
statements answered) = _____
Average score for this section

Transfer your score to the Reference
Architectures Index at the beginning of
the Self-Assessment.

CRITERION #6: CONTROL:

INTENT: Implement the practical solution. Maintain the performance and correct possible complications.

In my belief, the answer to this question is clearly defined:

5 Strongly Agree

4 Agree

3 Neutral

2 Disagree

1 Strongly Disagree

1. What are the key elements of your Reference Architectures performance improvement system, including your evaluation, organizational learning, and innovation processes?
<--- Score

2. Who will be in control?
<--- Score

3. What are your results for key measures or indicators of the accomplishment of your Reference Architectures strategy and action plans, including building and strengthening core competencies?
<--- Score

4. How can you best use all of your knowledge repositories to enhance learning and sharing?
<--- Score

5. Are suggested corrective/restorative actions indicated on the response plan for known causes to problems that might surface?
<--- Score

6. Do you monitor the effectiveness of your Reference Architectures activities?
<--- Score

7. How will you measure your QA plan's effectiveness?
<--- Score

8. How will report readings be checked to effectively monitor performance?
<--- Score

9. Are the planned controls in place?
<--- Score

10. You may have created your quality measures at a time when you lacked resources, technology wasn't up to the required standard, or low service levels were the industry norm. Have those circumstances changed?
<--- Score

11. Who controls critical resources?
<--- Score

12. How is Reference Architectures project cost planned, managed, monitored?
<--- Score

13. Who is the Reference Architectures process owner?
<--- Score

14. Does Reference Architectures appropriately measure and monitor risk?
<--- Score

15. Can you adapt and adjust to changing Reference Architectures situations?
<--- Score

16. Is a response plan in place for when the input, process, or output measures indicate an 'out-of-control' condition?
<--- Score

17. Can support from partners be adjusted?
<--- Score

18. What do you measure to verify effectiveness gains?
<--- Score

19. Are the planned controls working?
<--- Score

20. Will existing staff require re-training, for example, to learn new business processes?

<--- Score

21. Is there a transfer of ownership and knowledge to process owner and process team tasked with the responsibilities.
<--- Score

22. Is a response plan established and deployed?
<--- Score

23. Do the Reference Architectures decisions you make today help people and the planet tomorrow?
<--- Score

24. What is the control/monitoring plan?
<--- Score

25. Is the Reference Architectures test/monitoring cost justified?
<--- Score

26. Are documented procedures clear and easy to follow for the operators?
<--- Score

27. Has the improved process and its steps been standardized?
<--- Score

28. What are you attempting to measure/monitor?
<--- Score

29. How widespread is its use?
<--- Score

30. How do you plan for the cost of succession?

<--- Score

31. Implementation Planning: is a pilot needed to test the changes before a full roll out occurs?
<--- Score

32. Is there a documented and implemented monitoring plan?
<--- Score

33. How might the group capture best practices and lessons learned so as to leverage improvements?
<--- Score

34. Is there a recommended audit plan for routine surveillance inspections of Reference Architectures's gains?
<--- Score

35. Has the Reference Architectures value of standards been quantified?
<--- Score

36. How do your controls stack up?
<--- Score

37. Where do ideas that reach policy makers and planners as proposals for Reference Architectures strengthening and reform actually originate?
<--- Score

38. Are you measuring, monitoring and predicting Reference Architectures activities to optimize operations and profitability, and enhancing outcomes?
<--- Score

39. Have new or revised work instructions resulted?
<--- Score

40. How will Reference Architectures decisions be made and monitored?
<--- Score

41. What should you measure to verify efficiency gains?
<--- Score

42. Does job training on the documented procedures need to be part of the process team's education and training?
<--- Score

43. Does the response plan contain a definite closed loop continual improvement scheme (e.g., plan-do-check-act)?
<--- Score

44. What Reference Architectures standards are applicable?
<--- Score

45. What is your theory of human motivation, and how does your compensation plan fit with that view?
<--- Score

46. How will input, process, and output variables be checked to detect for sub-optimal conditions?
<--- Score

47. How do you select, collect, align, and integrate Reference Architectures data and information for

tracking daily operations and overall organizational performance, including progress relative to strategic objectives and action plans?
<--- Score

48. What are the known security controls?
<--- Score

49. What can you control?
<--- Score

50. Will any special training be provided for results interpretation?
<--- Score

51. How do you establish and deploy modified action plans if circumstances require a shift in plans and rapid execution of new plans?
<--- Score

52. Will the team be available to assist members in planning investigations?
<--- Score

53. Are controls in place and consistently applied?
<--- Score

54. In the case of a Reference Architectures project, the criteria for the audit derive from implementation objectives, an audit of a Reference Architectures project involves assessing whether the recommendations outlined for implementation have been met, can you track that any Reference Architectures project is implemented as planned, and is it working?
<--- Score

55. Act/Adjust: What Do you Need to Do Differently?
<--- Score

56. How will the process owner verify improvement in present and future sigma levels, process capabilities?
<--- Score

57. What other systems, operations, processes, and infrastructures (hiring practices, staffing, training, incentives/rewards, metrics/dashboards/scorecards, etc.) need updates, additions, changes, or deletions in order to facilitate knowledge transfer and improvements?
<--- Score

58. How do you spread information?
<--- Score

59. Is there an action plan in case of emergencies?
<--- Score

60. Are the Reference Architectures standards challenging?
<--- Score

61. How likely is the current Reference Architectures plan to come in on schedule or on budget?
<--- Score

62. Is there a standardized process?
<--- Score

63. How will new or emerging customer needs/requirements be checked/communicated to orient the process toward meeting the new specifications

and continually reducing variation?
<--- Score

64. What key inputs and outputs are being measured on an ongoing basis?
<--- Score

65. What quality tools were useful in the control phase?
<--- Score

66. Are operating procedures consistent?
<--- Score

67. Is knowledge gained on process shared and institutionalized?
<--- Score

68. How is change control managed?
<--- Score

69. Is there a control plan in place for sustaining improvements (short and long-term)?
<--- Score

70. What adjustments to the strategies are needed?
<--- Score

71. What are the critical parameters to watch?
<--- Score

72. What is your plan to assess your security risks?
<--- Score

73. Are new process steps, standards, and documentation ingrained into normal operations?

<--- Score

74. Are there documented procedures?
<--- Score

75. What do you stand for--and what are you against?
<--- Score

76. Do you monitor the Reference Architectures decisions made and fine tune them as they evolve?
<--- Score

77. How do controls support value?
<--- Score

78. Does the Reference Architectures performance meet the customer's requirements?
<--- Score

79. How will the process owner and team be able to hold the gains?
<--- Score

80. How will the day-to-day responsibilities for monitoring and continual improvement be transferred from the improvement team to the process owner?
<--- Score

81. How do you encourage people to take control and responsibility?
<--- Score

82. What is the standard for acceptable Reference Architectures performance?
<--- Score

83. What should the next improvement project be that is related to Reference Architectures?
<--- Score

84. Is new knowledge gained imbedded in the response plan?
<--- Score

85. Is reporting being used or needed?
<--- Score

86. What are customers monitoring?
<--- Score

87. Who sets the Reference Architectures standards?
<--- Score

88. Is there documentation that will support the successful operation of the improvement?
<--- Score

89. Does a troubleshooting guide exist or is it needed?
<--- Score

90. What is the best design framework for Reference Architectures organization now that, in a post industrial-age if the top-down, command and control model is no longer relevant?
<--- Score

91. How do you monitor usage and cost?
<--- Score

92. What is the recommended frequency of auditing?
<--- Score

93. What other areas of the group might benefit from the Reference Architectures team's improvements, knowledge, and learning?
<--- Score

94. Who has control over resources?
<--- Score

95. Is there a Reference Architectures Communication plan covering who needs to get what information when?
<--- Score

Add up total points for this section:
_____ = Total points for this section

Divided by: _____ (number of statements answered) = _____
Average score for this section

Transfer your score to the Reference Architectures Index at the beginning of the Self-Assessment.

CRITERION #7: SUSTAIN:

INTENT: Retain the benefits.

In my belief, the answer to this question is clearly defined:

5 Strongly Agree

4 Agree

3 Neutral

2 Disagree

1 Strongly Disagree

1. What unique value proposition (UVP) do you offer?
<--- Score

2. Who do you want your customers to become?
<--- Score

3. Is it economical; do you have the time and money?
<--- Score

4. What are you challenging?
<--- Score

5. What are the short and long-term Reference Architectures goals?
<--- Score

6. What is an unauthorized commitment?
<--- Score

7. How do you set Reference Architectures stretch targets and how do you get people to not only participate in setting these stretch targets but also that they strive to achieve these?
<--- Score

8. Do you have the right capabilities and capacities?
<--- Score

9. What are the barriers to increased Reference Architectures production?
<--- Score

10. What do your reports reflect?
<--- Score

11. How do you deal with Reference Architectures changes?
<--- Score

12. Which individuals, teams or departments will be involved in Reference Architectures?
<--- Score

13. Who is responsible for errors?
<--- Score

14. Would you rather sell to knowledgeable and

informed customers or to uninformed customers?
<--- Score

15. What is the source of the strategies for Reference
Architectures strengthening and reform?
<--- Score

16. How do you foster the skills, knowledge, talents,
attributes, and characteristics you want to have?
<--- Score

17. How do you determine the key elements that
affect Reference Architectures workforce satisfaction,
how are these elements determined for different
workforce groups and segments?
<--- Score

18. How do you create buy-in?
<--- Score

19. What are the potential basics of Reference
Architectures fraud?
<--- Score

20. Are you using a design thinking approach and
integrating Innovation, Reference Architectures
Experience, and Brand Value?
<--- Score

21. Will it be accepted by users?
<--- Score

22. Who will determine interim and final deadlines?
<--- Score

23. Is there any reason to believe the opposite of my

current belief?
<--- Score

24. How do you provide a safe environment
-physically and emotionally?
<--- Score

25. What trouble can you get into?
<--- Score

26. Who is responsible for Reference Architectures?
<--- Score

27. Who are your customers?
<--- Score

28. What may be the consequences for the
performance of an organization if all stakeholders are
not consulted regarding Reference Architectures?
<--- Score

29. What role does communication play in the success
or failure of a Reference Architectures project?
<--- Score

30. What happens at your organization when people
fail?
<--- Score

31. If no one would ever find out about your
accomplishments, how would you lead differently?
<--- Score

32. Did your employees make progress today?
<--- Score

33. Do you think Reference Architectures accomplishes the goals you expect it to accomplish?
<--- Score

34. What are the top 3 things at the forefront of your Reference Architectures agendas for the next 3 years?
<--- Score

35. Is the Reference Architectures organization completing tasks effectively and efficiently?
<--- Score

36. What counts that you are not counting?
<--- Score

37. If you had to leave your organization for a year and the only communication you could have with employees/colleagues was a single paragraph, what would you write?
<--- Score

38. Who do we want your customers to become?
<--- Score

39. How much contingency will be available in the budget?
<--- Score

40. How do you lead with Reference Architectures in mind?
<--- Score

41. Is your strategy driving your strategy? Or is the way in which you allocate resources driving your strategy?
<--- Score

42. What is the funding source for this project?
<--- Score

43. How do you know if you are successful?
<--- Score

44. What must you excel at?
<--- Score

45. What happens if you do not have enough
funding?
<--- Score

46. Which functions and people interact with the
supplier and or customer?
<--- Score

47. What is the range of capabilities?
<--- Score

48. Can you maintain your growth without detracting
from the factors that have contributed to your
success?
<--- Score

49. Ask yourself: how would you do this work if you
only had one staff member to do it?
<--- Score

50. What is effective Reference Architectures?
<--- Score

51. Who are four people whose careers you have
enhanced?
<--- Score

52. How do you stay inspired?
<--- Score

53. How will you ensure you get what you expected?
<--- Score

54. What happens when a new employee joins the organization?
<--- Score

55. In a project to restructure Reference Architectures outcomes, which stakeholders would you involve?
<--- Score

56. Why is Reference Architectures important for you now?
<--- Score

57. If you got fired and a new hire took your place, what would she do different?
<--- Score

58. How do you go about securing Reference Architectures?
<--- Score

59. What are you trying to prove to yourself, and how might it be hijacking your life and business success?
<--- Score

60. What are the key enablers to make this Reference Architectures move?
<--- Score

61. Is maximizing Reference Architectures protection

the same as minimizing Reference Architectures loss?
<--- Score

62. How do you foster innovation?
<--- Score

63. Why will customers want to buy your
organizations products/services?
<--- Score

64. Do you see more potential in people than they do
in themselves?
<--- Score

65. What should you stop doing?
<--- Score

66. What information is critical to your organization
that your executives are ignoring?
<--- Score

67. Who else should you help?
<--- Score

68. If there were zero limitations, what would you do
differently?
<--- Score

69. What you are going to do to affect the numbers?
<--- Score

70. Is your basic point _____ or _____?
<--- Score

71. What was the last experiment you ran?
<--- Score

72. What projects are going on in the organization today, and what resources are those projects using from the resource pools?
<--- Score

73. What are strategies for increasing support and reducing opposition?
<--- Score

74. To whom do you add value?
<--- Score

75. What does your signature ensure?
<--- Score

76. Instead of going to current contacts for new ideas, what if you reconnected with dormant contacts-- the people you used to know? If you were going reactivate a dormant tie, who would it be?
<--- Score

77. What Reference Architectures skills are most important?
<--- Score

78. What did you miss in the interview for the worst hire you ever made?
<--- Score

79. When information truly is ubiquitous, when reach and connectivity are completely global, when computing resources are infinite, and when a whole new set of impossibilities are not only possible, but happening, what will that do to your business?
<--- Score

80. Do you have an implicit bias for capital investments over people investments?
<--- Score

81. What management system can you use to leverage the Reference Architectures experience, ideas, and concerns of the people closest to the work to be done?
<--- Score

82. Is there a work around that you can use?
<--- Score

83. If you weren't already in this business, would you enter it today? And if not, what are you going to do about it?
<--- Score

84. How do you ensure that implementations of Reference Architectures products are done in a way that ensures safety?
<--- Score

85. Who uses your product in ways you never expected?
<--- Score

86. What would you recommend your friend do if he/she were facing this dilemma?
<--- Score

87. What are the essentials of internal Reference Architectures management?
<--- Score

88. If your customer were your grandmother, would you tell her to buy what you're selling?
<--- Score

89. How do you transition from the baseline to the target?
<--- Score

90. Where can you break convention?
<--- Score

91. In retrospect, of the projects that you pulled the plug on, what percent do you wish had been allowed to keep going, and what percent do you wish had ended earlier?
<--- Score

92. Do you feel that more should be done in the Reference Architectures area?
<--- Score

93. Do you say no to customers for no reason?
<--- Score

94. Who will be responsible for deciding whether Reference Architectures goes ahead or not after the initial investigations?
<--- Score

95. How do you listen to customers to obtain actionable information?
<--- Score

96. What are the gaps in your knowledge and experience?
<--- Score

97. What trophy do you want on your mantle?
<--- Score

98. How do senior leaders deploy your organizations vision and values through your leadership system, to the workforce, to key suppliers and partners, and to customers and other stakeholders, as appropriate?
<--- Score

99. What is your competitive advantage?
<--- Score

100. How can you negotiate Reference Architectures successfully with a stubborn boss, an irate client, or a deceitful coworker?
<--- Score

101. Whose voice (department, ethnic group, women, older workers, etc) might you have missed hearing from in your company, and how might you amplify this voice to create positive momentum for your business?
<--- Score

102. How do you engage the workforce, in addition to satisfying them?
<--- Score

103. How likely is it that a customer would recommend your company to a friend or colleague?
<--- Score

104. What are your personal philosophies regarding Reference Architectures and how do they influence your work?

<--- Score

105. What is the recommended frequency of auditing?
<--- Score

106. Whom among your colleagues do you trust, and for what?
<--- Score

107. How do you govern and fulfill your societal responsibilities?
<--- Score

108. Are assumptions made in Reference Architectures stated explicitly?
<--- Score

109. What are internal and external Reference Architectures relations?
<--- Score

110. How do you track customer value, profitability or financial return, organizational success, and sustainability?
<--- Score

111. Why not do Reference Architectures?
<--- Score

112. Is there any existing Reference Architectures governance structure?
<--- Score

113. What new services of functionality will be implemented next with Reference Architectures ?
<--- Score

114. What one word do you want to own in the minds of your customers, employees, and partners?
<--- Score

115. Which models, tools and techniques are necessary?
<--- Score

116. Which Reference Architectures goals are the most important?
<--- Score

117. What stupid rule would you most like to kill?
<--- Score

118. What is the overall talent health of your organization as a whole at senior levels, and for each organization reporting to a member of the Senior Leadership Team?
<--- Score

119. Are the criteria for selecting recommendations stated?
<--- Score

120. What are your most important goals for the strategic Reference Architectures objectives?
<--- Score

121. How do you make it meaningful in connecting Reference Architectures with what users do day-to-day?
<--- Score

122. Who is responsible for ensuring appropriate

resources (time, people and money) are allocated to Reference Architectures?
<--- Score

123. How do you keep the momentum going?
<--- Score

124. How do you manage Reference Architectures Knowledge Management (KM)?
<--- Score

125. What is your Reference Architectures strategy?
<--- Score

126. What could happen if you do not do it?
<--- Score

127. Who are the key stakeholders?
<--- Score

128. Marketing budgets are tighter, consumers are more skeptical, and social media has changed forever the way we talk about Reference Architectures, how do you gain traction?
<--- Score

129. What are the success criteria that will indicate that Reference Architectures objectives have been met and the benefits delivered?
<--- Score

130. What goals did you miss?
<--- Score

131. Will there be any necessary staff changes (redundancies or new hires)?

<--- Score

132. What is a feasible sequencing of reform initiatives over time?
<--- Score

133. Think of your Reference Architectures project, what are the main functions?
<--- Score

134. If you do not follow, then how to lead?
<--- Score

135. What are current Reference Architectures paradigms?
<--- Score

136. Can the schedule be done in the given time?
<--- Score

137. What Reference Architectures modifications can you make work for you?
<--- Score

138. Why is it important to have senior management support for a Reference Architectures project?
<--- Score

139. What are the business goals Reference Architectures is aiming to achieve?
<--- Score

140. Who is on the team?
<--- Score

141. What will be the consequences to the

stakeholder (financial, reputation etc) if Reference Architectures does not go ahead or fails to deliver the objectives?
<--- Score

142. How do you accomplish your long range Reference Architectures goals?
<--- Score

143. What business benefits will Reference Architectures goals deliver if achieved?
<--- Score

144. Is Reference Architectures realistic, or are you setting yourself up for failure?
<--- Score

145. How do customers see your organization?
<--- Score

146. What is the craziest thing you can do?
<--- Score

147. What is the purpose of Reference Architectures in relation to the mission?
<--- Score

148. How is implementation research currently incorporated into each of your goals?
<--- Score

149. What is it like to work for you?
<--- Score

150. Why should people listen to you?
<--- Score

151. What potential megatrends could make your business model obsolete?

<--- Score

152. Do you think you know, or do you know you know ?

<--- Score

153. Operational - will it work?

<--- Score

154. Are all key stakeholders present at all Structured Walkthroughs?

<--- Score

155. What have you done to protect your business from competitive encroachment?

<--- Score

156. Who have you, as a company, historically been when you've been at your best?

<--- Score

157. What is your question? Why?

<--- Score

158. How long will it take to change?

<--- Score

159. Reference architectures and Scrum: friends or foes?

<--- Score

160. How are you doing compared to your industry?

<--- Score

161. Do you have past Reference Architectures successes?
<--- Score

162. What are the long-term Reference Architectures goals?
<--- Score

163. How can you become the company that would put you out of business?
<--- Score

164. What relationships among Reference Architectures trends do you perceive?
<--- Score

165. Who, on the executive team or the board, has spoken to a customer recently?
<--- Score

166. What are the challenges?
<--- Score

167. How do you proactively clarify deliverables and Reference Architectures quality expectations?
<--- Score

168. Why do and why don't your customers like your organization?
<--- Score

169. What is something you believe that nearly no one agrees with you on?
<--- Score

170. How can you incorporate support to ensure safe and effective use of Reference Architectures into the services that you provide?
<--- Score

171. How can you become more high-tech but still be high touch?
<--- Score

172. If your company went out of business tomorrow, would anyone who doesn't get a paycheck here care?
<--- Score

173. What would have to be true for the option on the table to be the best possible choice?
<--- Score

174. Are you maintaining a past–present–future perspective throughout the Reference Architectures discussion?
<--- Score

175. How do you maintain Reference Architectures's Integrity?
<--- Score

176. At what moment would you think; Will I get fired?
<--- Score

177. Who is the main stakeholder, with ultimate responsibility for driving Reference Architectures forward?
<--- Score

178. Are the assumptions believable and achievable?
<--- Score

179. How will you motivate the stakeholders with the least vested interest?
<--- Score

180. Political -is anyone trying to undermine this project?
<--- Score

181. What have been your experiences in defining long range Reference Architectures goals?
<--- Score

182. Can you do all this work?
<--- Score

183. Who do you think the world wants your organization to be?
<--- Score

184. In the past year, what have you done (or could you have done) to increase the accurate perception of your company/brand as ethical and honest?
<--- Score

185. Are you / should you be revolutionary or evolutionary?
<--- Score

186. What is the overall business strategy?
<--- Score

187. Do you have enough freaky customers in your portfolio pushing you to the limit day in and day out?
<--- Score

188. How do you keep records, of what?
<--- Score

189. Are you making progress, and are you making progress as Reference Architectures leaders?
<--- Score

Add up total points for this section:
_ _ _ _ _ = Total points for this section

Divided by: _ _ _ _ _ _ (number of statements answered) = _ _ _ _ _ _
Average score for this section

Transfer your score to the Reference Architectures Index at the beginning of the Self-Assessment.

Reference Architectures and Managing Projects, Criteria for Project Managers:

1.0 Initiating Process Group: Reference Architectures

1. What are the constraints?

2. Who are the Reference Architectures project stakeholders?

3. In which Reference Architectures project management process group is the detailed Reference Architectures project budget created?

4. Do you understand the quality and control criteria that must be achieved for successful Reference Architectures project completion?

5. Do you understand the communication expectations for this Reference Architectures project?

6. Does it make any difference if you am successful?

7. Will the Reference Architectures project meet the client requirements, and will it achieve the business success criteria that justified doing the Reference Architectures project in the first place?

8. Did you use a contractor or vendor?

9. Mitigate. what will you do to minimize the impact should the risk event occur?

10. Did the Reference Architectures project team have the right skills?

11. What is the NEXT thing to do?

12. For technology Reference Architectures projects only: Are all production support stakeholders (Business unit, technical support, & user) prepared for implementation with appropriate contingency plans?

13. Who is performing the work of the Reference Architectures project?

14. Specific - is the objective clear in terms of what, how, when, and where the situation will be changed?

15. Are you properly tracking the progress of the Reference Architectures project and communicating the status to stakeholders?

16. If the risk event occurs, what will you do?

17. The Reference Architectures project managers have maximum authority in which type of organization?

18. What are the overarching issues of your organization?

19. How should needs be met?

20. Were decisions made in a timely manner?

1.1 Project Charter: Reference Architectures

21. Name and describe the elements that deal with providing the detail?

22. Who is the sponsor?

23. Pop quiz – which are the same inputs as in the Reference Architectures project charter?

24. What material?

25. What metrics could you look at?

26. How will you know that a change is an improvement?

27. What are the assumptions?

28. Why Outsource?

29. Customer benefits: what customer requirements does this Reference Architectures project address?

30. Why have you chosen the aim you have set forth?

31. Why is a Reference Architectures project Charter used?

32. Review the general mission What system will be affected by the improvement efforts?

33. Is time of the essence?

34. Will this replace an existing product?

35. Are you building in-house ?

36. Did your Reference Architectures project ask for this?

37. What are you striving to accomplish (measurable goal(s))?

38. How do you manage integration?

1.2 Stakeholder Register: Reference Architectures

39. What opportunities exist to provide communications?

40. What is the power of the stakeholder?

41. How much influence do they have on the Reference Architectures project?

42. Is your organization ready for change?

43. How should employers make voices heard?

44. How big is the gap?

45. Who are the stakeholders?

46. What & Why?

47. Who wants to talk about Security?

48. What are the major Reference Architectures project milestones requiring communications or providing communications opportunities?

49. How will reports be created?

50. Who is managing stakeholder engagement?

1.3 Stakeholder Analysis Matrix: Reference Architectures

51. What unique or lowest-cost resources does the Reference Architectures project have access to?

52. What do you need to appraise?

53. How do rules, behaviors affect stakes?

54. Are there people who ise voices or interests in the issue may not be heard?

55. How does the Reference Architectures project involve consultations or collaboration with other organizations?

56. What tools would help you communicate?

57. What is the stakeholders mandate, what is mission?

58. What is the issue at stake?

59. Who will obstruct/hinder the Reference Architectures project if they are not involved?

60. How will the Reference Architectures project benefit them?

61. Disadvantages of proposition?

62. Has there been a similar initiative in the region?

63. Timescales, deadlines and pressures?

64. Who has not been involved up to now and should have been?

65. Who can contribute financial or technical resources towards the work?

66. Geographical, export, import?

67. Who will be responsible for managing the outcome?

68. How are you predicting what future (work)loads will be?

69. Technology development and innovation?

70. What organizational arrangements are planned to ensure the Reference Architectures project achieves its social development outcomes?

2.0 Planning Process Group: Reference Architectures

71. How will users learn how to use the deliverables?

72. What do they need to know about the Reference Architectures project?

73. What are the different approaches to building the WBS?

74. Professionals want to know what is expected from them; what are the deliverables?

75. Why is it important to determine activity sequencing on Reference Architectures projects?

76. How will it affect you?

77. In which Reference Architectures project management process group is the detailed Reference Architectures project budget created?

78. In what way has the program contributed towards the issue culture and development included on the public agenda?

79. Are you just doing busywork to pass the time?

80. If task x starts two days late, what is the effect on the Reference Architectures project end date?

81. First of all, should any action be taken?

82. Is the schedule for the set products being met?

83. Is the Reference Architectures project making progress in helping to achieve the set results?

84. When developing the estimates for Reference Architectures project phases, you choose to add the individual estimates for the activities that comprise each phase. What type of estimation method are you using?

85. How are the principles of aid effectiveness (ownership, alignment, management for development results and mutual responsibility) being applied in the Reference Architectures project?

86. What good practices or successful experiences or transferable examples have been identified?

87. How are it Reference Architectures projects different?

88. To what extent and in what ways are the Reference Architectures project contributing to progress towards organizational reform?

89. Are the necessary foundations in place to ensure the sustainability of the results of the Reference Architectures project?

90. How can you make your needs known?

2.1 Project Management Plan: Reference Architectures

91. When is a Reference Architectures project management plan created?

92. What is the justification?

93. Development trends and opportunities. What if the positive direction and vision of your organization causes expected trends to change?

94. How well are you able to manage your risk?

95. Who manages integration?

96. Has the selected plan been formulated using cost effectiveness and incremental analysis techniques?

97. Are there non-structural buyout or relocation recommendations?

98. Is mitigation authorized or recommended?

99. Do there need to be organizational changes?

100. How do you organize the costs in the Reference Architectures project management plan?

101. Is the budget realistic?

102. When is the Reference Architectures project management plan created?

103. Are there any client staffing expectations?

104. Is the appropriate plan selected based on your organizations objectives and evaluation criteria expressed in Principles and Guidelines policies?

105. What does management expect of PMs?

106. Do the proposed changes from the Reference Architectures project include any significant risks to safety?

107. What should you drop in order to add something new?

108. How can you best help your organization to develop consistent practices in Reference Architectures project management planning stages?

2.2 Scope Management Plan: Reference Architectures

109. Are the payment terms being followed?

110. Is it possible to track all classes of Reference Architectures project work (e.g. scheduled, un-scheduled, defect repair, etc.)?

111. Are any non-compliance issues that exist due to organizations practices?

112. Materials available for performing the work?

113. Is there general agreement & acceptance of the current status and progress of the Reference Architectures project?

114. Describe the process for rejecting the Reference Architectures project deliverables. What happens to rejected deliverables?

115. Given the scope of the Reference Architectures project, which criterion should be optimized?

116. Have adequate procedures been put in place for Reference Architectures project communication and status reporting across Reference Architectures project boundaries (for example interdependent software development among interfacing systems)?

117. Is there a requirements change management processes in place?

118. Are funding resource estimates sufficiently detailed and documented for use in planning and tracking the Reference Architectures project?

119. Is the quality assurance team identified?

120. Have all team members been part of identifying risks?

121. Are alternatives safe, functional, constructible, economical, reasonable and sustainable?

122. What does the critical path really mean?

123. Are you spending the right amount of money for specific tasks?

124. Is there a scope management plan that includes how Reference Architectures project scope will be defined, developed, monitored, validated and controlled?

125. Alignment to strategic goals & objectives?

126. Are issues raised, assessed, actioned, and resolved in a timely and efficient manner?

127. What work performance data will be captured?

128. Are metrics used to evaluate and manage Vendors?

2.3 Requirements Management Plan: Reference Architectures

129. What are you counting on?

130. Does the Reference Architectures project have a Change Control process?

131. How knowledgeable is the primary Stakeholder(s) in the proposed application area?

132. What is the earliest finish date for this Reference Architectures project if it is scheduled to start on ...?

133. How often will the reporting occur?

134. Is there formal agreement on who has authority to approve a change in requirements?

135. Will the product release be stable and mature enough to be deployed in the user community?

136. What went right?

137. What cost metrics will be used?

138. How will the requirements become prioritized?

139. Have stakeholders been instructed in the Change Control process?

140. In case of software development; Should you have a test for each code module?

141. Do you have an agreed upon process for alerting the Reference Architectures project Manager if a request for change in requirements leads to a product scope change?

142. Will you perform a Requirements Risk assessment and develop a plan to deal with risks?

143. Is there formal agreement on who has authority to request a change in requirements?

144. How do you know that you have done this right?

145. Do you expect stakeholders to be cooperative?

146. Do you really need to write this document at all?

147. Is the user satisfied?

148. Who is responsible for quantifying the Reference Architectures project requirements?

2.4 Requirements Documentation: Reference Architectures

149. How much does requirements engineering cost?

150. Can the requirement be changed without a large impact on other requirements?

151. Do your constraints stand?

152. What is the risk associated with cost and schedule?

153. What is your Elevator Speech?

154. Are there legal issues?

155. How can you document system requirements?

156. Is the origin of the requirement clearly stated?

157. Are there any requirements conflicts?

158. How will the proposed Reference Architectures project help?

159. Validity. does the system provide the functions which best support the customers needs?

160. Who is interacting with the system?

161. Is the requirement realistically testable?

162. How does what is being described meet the business need?

163. What are the attributes of a customer?

164. Basic work/business process; high-level, what is being touched?

165. What variations exist for a process?

166. How will they be documented / shared?

167. Has requirements gathering uncovered information that would necessitate changes?

2.5 Requirements Traceability Matrix: Reference Architectures

168. Describe the process for approving requirements so they can be added to the traceability matrix and Reference Architectures project work can be performed. Will the Reference Architectures project requirements become approved in writing?

169. What percentage of Reference Architectures projects are producing traceability matrices between requirements and other work products?

170. Why use a WBS?

171. How small is small enough?

172. Is there a requirements traceability process in place?

173. How will it affect the stakeholders personally in career?

174. Will you use a Requirements Traceability Matrix?

175. Do you have a clear understanding of all subcontracts in place?

176. How do you manage scope?

177. What are the chronologies, contingencies, consequences, criteria?

178. Why do you manage scope?

179. What is the WBS?

2.6 Project Scope Statement: Reference Architectures

180. Where and how does the team fit within your organization structure?

181. Were potential customers involved early in the planning process?

182. Why do you need to manage scope?

183. Has a method and process for requirement tracking been developed?

184. Is the Reference Architectures project manager qualified and experienced in Reference Architectures project management?

185. Is the Reference Architectures project organization documented and on file?

186. If the scope changes, what will the impact be to your Reference Architectures project in terms of duration, cost, quality, or any other important areas of the Reference Architectures project?

187. Elements that deal with providing the detail?

188. Which risks does the Reference Architectures project focus on?

189. Will all tasks resulting from issues be entered into the Reference Architectures project Plan and tracked

through the plan?

190. Were key Reference Architectures project stakeholders brought into the Reference Architectures project Plan?

191. Is this process communicated to the customer and team members?

192. Are there backup strategies for key members of the Reference Architectures project?

193. Is the plan for your organization of the Reference Architectures project resources adequate?

194. Is there a baseline plan against which to measure progress?

195. Elements of scope management that deal with concept development ?

196. Has the Reference Architectures project scope statement been reviewed as part of the baseline process?

197. Are there completion/verification criteria defined for each task producing an output?

2.7 Assumption and Constraint Log: Reference Architectures

198. What if failure during recovery?

199. Contradictory information between different documents?

200. Should factors be unpredictable over time?

201. After observing execution of process, is it in compliance with the documented Plan?

202. Were the system requirements formally reviewed prior to initiating the design phase?

203. What strengths do you have?

204. Is this model reasonable?

205. If it is out of compliance, should the process be amended or should the Plan be amended?

206. How are new requirements or changes to requirements identified?

207. Is staff trained on the software technologies that are being used on the Reference Architectures project?

208. Is the steering committee active in Reference Architectures project oversight?

209. Is the process working, and people are not executing in compliance of the process?

210. Are there ways to reduce the time it takes to get something approved?

211. Are processes for release management of new development from coding and unit testing, to integration testing, to training, and production defined and followed?

212. Is the definition of the Reference Architectures project scope clear; what needs to be accomplished?

213. How can you prevent/fix violations?

214. What to do at recovery?

215. Has a Reference Architectures project Communications Plan been developed?

216. Is there adequate stakeholder participation for the vetting of requirements definition, changes and management?

217. What weaknesses do you have?

2.8 Work Breakdown Structure: Reference Architectures

218. Where does it take place?

219. How will you and your Reference Architectures project team define the Reference Architectures projects scope and work breakdown structure?

220. Is the work breakdown structure (wbs) defined and is the scope of the Reference Architectures project clear with assigned deliverable owners?

221. How far down?

222. Can you make it?

223. How big is a work-package?

224. Who has to do it?

225. Do you need another level?

226. What is the probability that the Reference Architectures project duration will exceed xx weeks?

227. When does it have to be done?

228. How much detail?

229. When do you stop?

230. When would you develop a Work Breakdown

Structure?

231. Is it still viable?

232. Is it a change in scope?

233. What has to be done?

234. What is the probability of completing the Reference Architectures project in less that xx days?

235. Why would you develop a Work Breakdown Structure?

2.9 WBS Dictionary: Reference Architectures

236. Is all contract work included in the CWBS?

237. Is cost performance measurement at the point in time most suitable for the category of material involved, and no earlier than the time of actual receipt of material?

238. Does the accounting system provide a basis for auditing records of direct costs chargeable to the contract?

239. What size should a work package be?

240. Does the scheduling system provide for the identification of work progress against technical and other milestones, and also provide for forecasts of completion dates of scheduled work?

241. Does the contractors system include procedures for measuring the performance of critical subcontractors?

242. Where learning is used in developing underlying budgets is there a direct relationship between anticipated learning and time phased budgets?

243. Are data elements reconcilable between internal summary reports and reports forwarded to us?

244. How many levels?

245. Are the contractors estimates of costs at completion reconcilable with cost data reported to us?

246. All cwbs elements specified for external reporting?

247. Are meaningful indicators identified for use in measuring the status of cost and schedule performance?

248. Should you have a test for each code module?

249. Is budgeted cost for work performed calculated in a manner consistent with the way work is planned?

250. Are the bases and rates for allocating costs from each indirect pool consistently applied?

251. Does the contractors system provide unit or lot costs when applicable?

252. Are retroactive changes to BCWS and BCWP prohibited except for correction of errors or for normal accounting adjustments?

253. Major functional areas of contract effort?

254. The Reference Architectures projected business base for each period?

255. Are the overhead pools formally and adequately identified?

2.10 Schedule Management Plan: Reference Architectures

256. What happens if a warning is triggered?

257. How are Reference Architectures projects different from operations?

258. Are updated Reference Architectures project time & resource estimates reasonable based on the current Reference Architectures project stage?

259. Reference Architectures project definition & scope?

260. Have all documents been archived in a Reference Architectures project repository for each release?

261. Have external dependencies been captured in the schedule?

262. Are the processes for status updates and maintenance defined?

263. Does the time Reference Architectures projection include an amount for contingencies (time reserves)?

264. Have all unresolved risks been documented?

265. Have key stakeholders been identified?

266. Why conduct schedule analysis?

267. Are assumptions being identified, recorded, analyzed, qualified and closed?

268. Are Reference Architectures project contact logs kept up to date?

269. Are the quality tools and methods identified in the Quality Plan appropriate to the Reference Architectures project?

270. List all schedule constraints here. Must the Reference Architectures project be complete by a specified date?

271. Are Reference Architectures project team members involved in detailed estimating and scheduling?

272. Is there a formal process for updating the Reference Architectures project baseline?

273. Is current scope of the Reference Architectures project substantially different than that originally defined?

2.11 Activity List: Reference Architectures

274. Who will perform the work?

275. Should you include sub-activities?

276. When will the work be performed?

277. What is your organizations history in doing similar activities?

278. When do the individual activities need to start and finish?

279. What went wrong?

280. Is there anything planned that does not need to be here?

281. For other activities, how much delay can be tolerated?

282. Where will it be performed?

283. How do you determine the late start (LS) for each activity?

284. How should ongoing costs be monitored to try to keep the Reference Architectures project within budget?

285. How can the Reference Architectures project be

displayed graphically to better visualize the activities?

286. How much slack is available in the Reference Architectures project?

287. The wbs is developed as part of a joint planning session. and how do you know that youhave done this right?

288. What will be performed?

289. In what sequence?

290. What is the probability the Reference Architectures project can be completed in xx weeks?

291. What went well?

292. Are the required resources available or need to be acquired?

2.12 Activity Attributes: Reference Architectures

293. Would you consider either of corresponding activities an outlier?

294. How many resources do you need to complete the work scope within a limit of X number of days?

295. Has management defined a definite timeframe for the turnaround or Reference Architectures project window?

296. Have constraints been applied to the start and finish milestones for the phases?

297. How many days do you need to complete the work scope with a limit of X number of resources?

298. Were there other ways you could have organized the data to achieve similar results?

299. How difficult will it be to complete specific activities on this Reference Architectures project?

300. How much activity detail is required?

301. What is missing?

302. Activity: fair or not fair?

303. Where else does it apply?

304. Resources to accomplish the work?

305. Can you re-assign any activities to another resource to resolve an over-allocation?

306. Which method produces the more accurate cost assignment?

307. Activity: what is Missing?

308. What is the general pattern here?

2.13 Milestone List: Reference Architectures

309. Loss of key staff?

310. Political effects?

311. Usps (unique selling points)?

312. How soon can the activity finish?

313. How will you get the word out to customers?

314. Describe the concept of the technology, product or service that will be or has been developed. How will it be used?

315. How late can each activity be finished and started?

316. Describe your organizations strengths and core competencies. What factors will make your organization succeed?

317. When will the Reference Architectures project be complete?

318. What specific improvements did you make to the Reference Architectures project proposal since the previous time?

319. What background experience, skills, and strengths does the team bring to your organization?

320. Marketing - reach, distribution, awareness?

321. Sustaining internal capabilities?

322. Describe the industry you are in and the market growth opportunities. What is the market for your technology, product or service?

323. Do you foresee any technical risks or developmental challenges?

324. New USPs?

325. Environmental effects?

326. Legislative effects?

327. Continuity, supply chain robustness?

2.14 Network Diagram: Reference Architectures

328. What is the probability of completing the Reference Architectures project in less that xx days?

329. What are the Major Administrative Issues?

330. Will crashing x weeks return more in benefits than it costs?

331. What job or jobs precede it?

332. Which type of network diagram allows you to depict four types of dependencies?

333. What activities must follow this activity?

334. What are the Key Success Factors?

335. Planning: who, how long, what to do?

336. What can be done concurrently?

337. Exercise: what is the probability that the Reference Architectures project duration will exceed xx weeks?

338. What is the completion time?

339. Review the logical flow of the network diagram. Take a look at which activities you have first and then sequence the activities. Do they make sense?

340. Can you calculate the confidence level?

341. What to do and When?

342. What job or jobs could run concurrently?

343. What are the tools?

344. If x is long, what would be the completion time if you break x into two parallel parts of y weeks and z weeks?

345. What controls the start and finish of a job?

2.15 Activity Resource Requirements: Reference Architectures

346. Why do you do that?

347. Organizational Applicability?

348. What is the Work Plan Standard?

349. Are there unresolved issues that need to be addressed?

350. How do you manage time?

351. What are constraints that you might find during the Human Resource Planning process?

352. When does monitoring begin?

353. Do you use tools like decomposition and rolling-wave planning to produce the activity list and other outputs?

354. How do you handle petty cash?

355. Anything else?

356. Which logical relationship does the PDM use most often?

357. Other support in specific areas?

358. How many signatures do you require on a

check and does this match what is in your policy and procedures?

359. Time for overtime?

2.16 Resource Breakdown Structure: Reference Architectures

360. What is the number one predictor of a groups productivity?

361. Changes based on input from stakeholders?

362. Is predictive resource analysis being done?

363. What defines a successful Reference Architectures project?

364. Who needs what information?

365. Which resources should be in the resource pool?

366. Who is allowed to see what data about which resources?

367. How can this help you with team building?

368. What can you do to improve productivity?

369. Who is allowed to perform which functions?

370. What is each stakeholders desired outcome for the Reference Architectures project?

371. Why is this important?

372. What defines a successful Reference Architectures project?

373. Who will be used as a Reference Architectures project team member?

374. Who will use the system?

375. Any changes from stakeholders?

376. What is the difference between % Complete and % work?

377. Why do you do it?

2.17 Activity Duration Estimates: Reference Architectures

378. What is done after activity duration estimation?

379. Are Reference Architectures project management tools and techniques consistently applied throughout all Reference Architectures projects?

380. Will outside resources be needed to help in its development?

381. Do they make sense?

382. How difficult will it be to complete specific activities on this Reference Architectures project?

383. If Reference Architectures project time and cost are not as important as the number of resources used each month, which is the BEST thing to do?

384. Is a Reference Architectures project charter created once a Reference Architectures project is formally recognized?

385. After changes are approved are Reference Architectures project documents updated and distributed?

386. What type of information goes in a quality assurance plan?

387. How could you use each technique in your

organization?

388. What type of contract was used and why?

389. Are procedures defined for calculating cost estimates?

390. What is the difference between conceptual, application, and evaluative questions?

391. Reference Architectures project manager is using weighted average duration estimates to perform schedule network analysis. Which type of mathematical analysis is being used?

392. Could it have been avoided?

393. Which is correct?

394. Do Reference Architectures project team members work in the same physical location to enhance team performance?

395. Are activity dependencies documented?

396. What does it mean to take a systems view of a Reference Architectures project?

2.18 Duration Estimating Worksheet: Reference Architectures

397. Is a construction detail attached (to aid in explanation)?

398. What is your role?

399. What is cost and Reference Architectures project cost management?

400. Is this operation cost effective?

401. What questions do you have?

402. When, then?

403. What info is needed?

404. Done before proceeding with this activity or what can be done concurrently?

405. Is the Reference Architectures project responsive to community need?

406. Can the Reference Architectures project be constructed as planned?

407. Value pocket identification & quantification what are value pockets?

408. What is an Average Reference Architectures project?

409. How can the Reference Architectures project be displayed graphically to better visualize the activities?

410. Do any colleagues have experience with your organization and/or RFPs?

411. Why estimate time and cost?

412. Small or large Reference Architectures project?

413. When does your organization expect to be able to complete it?

414. Science = process: remember the scientific method?

415. How should ongoing costs be monitored to try to keep the Reference Architectures project within budget?

2.19 Project Schedule: Reference Architectures

416. Why do you need to manage Reference Architectures project Risk?

417. Are there activities that came from a template or previous Reference Architectures project that are not applicable on this phase of this Reference Architectures project?

418. How do you use schedules?

419. How do you manage Reference Architectures project Risk?

420. What does that mean?

421. Are procedures defined by which the Reference Architectures project schedule may be changed?

422. What documents, if any, will the subcontractor provide (eg Reference Architectures project schedule, quality plan etc)?

423. What is risk?

424. If there are any qualifying green components to this Reference Architectures project, what portion of the total Reference Architectures project cost is green?

425. How do you know that youhave done this right?

426. Change management required?

427. Are quality inspections and review activities listed in the Reference Architectures project schedule(s)?

428. Are the original Reference Architectures project schedule and budget realistic?

429. Your best shot for providing estimations how complex/how much work does the activity require?

430. Is the structure for tracking the Reference Architectures project schedule well defined and assigned to a specific individual?

431. Reference Architectures project work estimates Who is managing the work estimate quality of work tasks in the Reference Architectures project schedule?

2.20 Cost Management Plan: Reference Architectures

432. Are the Reference Architectures project team members located locally to the users/stakeholders?

433. Are quality inspections and review activities listed in the Reference Architectures project schedule(s)?

434. Are updated Reference Architectures project time & resource estimates reasonable based on the current Reference Architectures project stage?

435. Has a capability assessment been conducted?

436. Who will prepare the cost estimates?

437. How do you manage cost?

438. Was your organizations estimating methodology being used and followed?

439. What is cost and Reference Architectures project cost management?

440. Is there a Steering Committee in place?

441. What is your organizations history in doing similar tasks?

442. Are Reference Architectures project leaders committed to this Reference Architectures project full

time?

443. Are meeting objectives identified for each meeting?

444. Have the key functions and capabilities been defined and assigned to each release or iteration?

445. What would you do differently what did not work?

446. Contractors scope – how will contractors scope be defined when contracts are let?

447. Is the Reference Architectures project sponsor clearly communicating the business case or rationale for why this Reference Architectures project is needed?

448. Who should write the PEP?

449. Are staff skills known and available for each task?

2.21 Activity Cost Estimates: Reference Architectures

450. What makes a good expected result statement?

451. Where can you get activity reports?

452. Maintenance Reserve?

453. Would you hire them again?

454. Will you use any tools, such as Reference Architectures project management software, to assist in capturing Earned Value metrics?

455. When do you enter into PPM?

456. Did the consultant work with local staff to develop local capacity?

457. Is there anything unique in this Reference Architectures projects scope statement that will affect resources?

458. What do you want to know about the stay to know if costs were inappropriately high or low?

459. What is the estimators estimating history?

460. How and when do you enter into Reference Architectures project Procurement Management?

461. Can you delete activities or make them inactive?

462. Does the estimator estimate by task or by person?

463. What is the activity recast of the budget?

464. Performance bond should always provide what part of the contract value?

465. How difficult will it be to do specific tasks on the Reference Architectures project?

466. What were things that you did well, and could improve, and how?

467. Will you need to provide essential services information about activities?

2.22 Cost Estimating Worksheet: Reference Architectures

468. Is the Reference Architectures project responsive to community need?

469. Identify the timeframe necessary to monitor progress and collect data to determine how the selected measure has changed?

470. Ask: are others positioned to know, are others credible, and will others cooperate?

471. What costs are to be estimated?

472. What additional Reference Architectures project(s) could be initiated as a result of this Reference Architectures project?

473. Will the Reference Architectures project collaborate with the local community and leverage resources?

474. What can be included?

475. What is the purpose of estimating?

476. Can a trend be established from historical performance data on the selected measure and are the criteria for using trend analysis or forecasting methods met?

477. What will others want?

478. Does the Reference Architectures project provide innovative ways for stakeholders to overcome obstacles or deliver better outcomes?

479. How will the results be shared and to whom?

480. What happens to any remaining funds not used?

481. Who is best positioned to know and assist in identifying corresponding factors?

482. Is it feasible to establish a control group arrangement?

483. What is the estimated labor cost today based upon this information?

2.23 Cost Baseline: Reference Architectures

484. Does it impact schedule, cost, quality?

485. Has the Reference Architectures project documentation been archived or otherwise disposed as described in the Reference Architectures project communication plan?

486. If you sold 10x widgets on a day, what would the affect on profits be?

487. Vac -variance at completion, how much over/ under budget do you expect to be?

488. Does the suggested change request seem to represent a necessary enhancement to the product?

489. Has the Reference Architectures projected annual cost to operate and maintain the product(s) or service(s) been approved and funded?

490. Are you asking management for something as a result of this update?

491. How long are you willing to wait before you find out were late?

492. Escalation criteria met?

493. Is there anything unique in this Reference Architectures projects scope statement that will affect

resources?

494. Have the lessons learned been filed with the Reference Architectures project Management Office?

495. Is the cr within Reference Architectures project scope?

496. Are you meeting with your team regularly?

497. Pcs for your new business. what would the life cycle costs be?

498. When should cost estimates be developed?

499. Impact to environment?

500. Eac -estimate at completion, what is the total job expected to cost?

2.24 Quality Management Plan: Reference Architectures

501. How does your organization ensure the quality, reliability, and user-friendliness of its hardware and software?

502. How does your organization manage training and evaluate its effectiveness?

503. How does your organization perform analyzes to assess overall organizational performance and set priorities?

504. Have all stakeholders been identified?

505. How are senior leaders, employees, and your organization involved in supporting the community?

506. Is there a procedure for this process?

507. Modifications to the requirements?

508. Does the system design reflect the requirements?

509. What changes can you make that will result in improvement?

510. How many Reference Architectures project staff does this specific process affect?

511. What has the QM Collaboration done?

512. What are the established criteria that sampling / testing data are compared against?

513. What would be the next steps or what else should you do at this point?

514. How do senior leaders create an environment that encourages learning and innovation?

515. What are the appropriate test methods to be used?

516. How is equipment calibrated?

517. Are qmps good forever?

518. Have all involved stakeholders and work groups committed to the Reference Architectures project?

519. How do your action plans support the strategic objectives?

520. What is the return on investment?

2.25 Quality Metrics: Reference Architectures

521. What do you measure?

522. Did evaluation start on time?

523. How do you communicate results and findings to upper management?

524. Do the operators focus on determining; is there anything you need to worry about?

525. Where is quality now?

526. Can you correlate your quality metrics to profitability?

527. Are there already quality metrics available that detect nonlinear embeddings and trends similar to the users perception?

528. Are documents on hand to provide explanations of privacy and confidentiality?

529. What is the timeline to meet your goal?

530. Where did complaints, returns and warranty claims come from?

531. What does this tell us?

532. How exactly do you define when differences

exist?

533. Was the overall quality better or worse than previous products?

534. What metrics do you measure?

535. Have risk areas been identified?

536. What documentation is required?

537. What happens if you get an abnormal result?

538. What are your organizations next steps?

539. What if the biggest risk to your business were the already stated people who do not complain?

2.26 Process Improvement Plan: Reference Architectures

540. Has a process guide to collect the data been developed?

541. What actions are needed to address the problems and achieve the goals?

542. Modeling current processes is great, and will you ever see a return on that investment?

543. Have storage and access mechanisms and procedures been determined?

544. Where do you focus?

545. To elicit goal statements, do you ask a question such as, What do you want to achieve?

546. What personnel are the champions for the initiative?

547. Have the supporting tools been developed or acquired?

548. Everyone agrees on what process improvement is, right?

549. Have the frequency of collection and the points in the process where measurements will be made been determined?

550. Where do you want to be?

551. Does explicit definition of the measures exist?

552. What lessons have you learned so far?

553. Are you making progress on the goals?

554. Who should prepare the process improvement action plan?

555. Does your process ensure quality?

556. The motive is determined by asking, Why do you want to achieve this goal?

557. Management commitment at all levels?

558. Are there forms and procedures to collect and record the data?

2.27 Responsibility Assignment Matrix: Reference Architectures

559. Which Reference Architectures project management knowledge area is least mature?

560. Evaluate the impact of schedule changes, work around, etc?

561. Are detailed work packages planned as far in advance as practicable?

562. Past experience – the person or the group worked at something similar in the past?

563. Are all authorized tasks assigned to identified organizational elements?

564. How do you assist them to be as productive as possible?

565. Do work packages consist of discrete tasks which are adequately described?

566. Incurrence of actual indirect costs in excess of budgets, by element of expense?

567. What tool can show you individual and group allocations?

568. What happens when others get pulled for higher priority Reference Architectures projects?

569. Are indirect costs accumulated for comparison with the corresponding budgets?

570. How do you manage remotely to staff in other Divisions?

571. With too many people labeled as doing the work, are there too many hands involved?

572. Is the anticipated (firm and potential) business base Reference Architectures projected in a rational, consistent manner?

573. When performing is split among two or more roles, is the work clearly defined so that the efforts are coordinated and the communication is clear?

574. How many hours by each staff member/rate?

575. Undistributed budgets, if any?

576. What is the purpose of assigning and documenting responsibility?

2.28 Roles and Responsibilities: Reference Architectures

577. What should you highlight for improvement?

578. What expectations were NOT met?

579. Be specific; avoid generalities. Thank you and great work alone are insufficient. What exactly do you appreciate and why?

580. Where are you most strong as a supervisor?

581. Implementation of actions: Who are the responsible units?

582. What should you do now to ensure that you are meeting all expectations of your current position?

583. Are the quality assurance functions and related roles and responsibilities clearly defined?

584. What expectations were met?

585. Required skills, knowledge, experience?

586. Are Reference Architectures project team roles and responsibilities identified and documented?

587. What should you do now to prepare yourself for a promotion, increased responsibilities or a different job?

588. What is working well within your organizations performance management system?

589. Are Reference Architectures project team roles and responsibilities identified and documented?

590. What specific behaviors did you observe?

591. Is feedback clearly communicated and non-judgmental?

592. What should you do now to prepare for your career 5+ years from now?

593. Key conclusions and recommendations: Are conclusions and recommendations relevant and acceptable?

594. How well did the Reference Architectures project Team understand the expectations of specific roles and responsibilities?

595. To decide whether to use a quality measurement, ask how will you know when it is achieved?

2.29 Human Resource Management Plan: Reference Architectures

596. Is there an on-going process in place to monitor Reference Architectures project risks?

597. Cost / benefit analysis?

598. Who is involved?

599. What did you have to assume to be true to complete the charter?

600. Are risk oriented checklists used during risk identification?

601. Is there general agreement & acceptance of the current status and progress of the Reference Architectures project?

602. Is the steering committee active in Reference Architectures project oversight?

603. Are Reference Architectures project team roles and responsibilities identified and documented?

604. Are the quality tools and methods identified in the Quality Plan appropriate to the Reference Architectures project?

605. Are procurement deliverables arriving on time and to specification?

606. Is your organization certified as a supplier, wholesaler, regular dealer, or manufacturer of corresponding products/supplies?

607. Are people being developed to meet the challenges of the future?

608. Is there a formal set of procedures supporting Issues Management?

609. Has the scope management document been updated and distributed to help prevent scope creep?

610. Are risk triggers captured?

611. How are you going to ensure that you have a well motivated workforce?

2.30 Communications Management Plan: Reference Architectures

612. Who were proponents/opponents?

613. Conflict resolution -which method when?

614. Is there an important stakeholder who is actively opposed and will not receive messages?

615. Why manage stakeholders?

616. Can you think of other people who might have concerns or interests?

617. How did the term stakeholder originate?

618. How is this initiative related to other portfolios, programs, or Reference Architectures projects?

619. Why do you manage communications?

620. How were corresponding initiatives successful?

621. Timing: when do the effects of the communication take place?

622. Who did you turn to if you had questions?

623. Who is the stakeholder?

624. What steps can you take for a positive relationship?

625. What approaches to you feel are the best ones to use?

626. Do you ask; can you recommend others for you to talk with about this initiative?

627. Are others part of the communications management plan?

628. Where do team members get information?

629. Who to share with?

630. Is the stakeholder role recognized by your organization?

2.31 Risk Management Plan: Reference Architectures

631. Costs associated with late delivery or a defective product?

632. Are team members trained in the use of the tools?

633. How well were you able to manage your risk before?

634. What are it-specific requirements?

635. Risk documentation: what reporting formats and processes will be used for risk management activities?

636. Are there new risks that mitigation strategies might introduce?

637. Is the necessary data being captured and is it complete and accurate?

638. Do you manage the process through use of metrics?

639. Are the reports useful and easy to read?

640. Does the customer have a solid idea of what is required?

641. Degree of confidence in estimated size estimate?

642. Are the required plans included, such as nonstructural flood risk management plans?

643. Can the Reference Architectures project proceed without assuming the risk?

644. Risk probability and impact: how will the probabilities and impacts of risk items be assessed?

645. Market risk -will the new service or product be useful to your organization or marketable to others?

646. How quickly does this item need to be resolved?

647. My Reference Architectures project leader has suddenly left your organization, what do you do?

648. Was an original risk assessment/risk management plan completed?

649. What things might go wrong?

2.32 Risk Register: Reference Architectures

650. Can the likelihood and impact of failing to achieve corresponding recommendations and action plans be assessed?

651. User involvement: do you have the right users?

652. How could corresponding Risk affect the Reference Architectures project in terms of cost and schedule?

653. What further options might be available for responding to the risk?

654. What can be done about it?

655. What is your current and future risk profile?

656. What would the impact to the Reference Architectures project objectives be should the risk arise?

657. What may happen or not go according to plan?

658. What should you do when?

659. Who needs to know about this?

660. Assume the risk event or situation happens, what would the impact be?

661. Assume the event happens, what is the Most Likely impact?

662. Have other controls and solutions been implemented in other services which could be applied as an alternative to additional funding?

663. How are risks graded?

664. Which key risks have ineffective responses or outstanding improvement actions?

665. Budget and schedule: what are the estimated costs and schedules for performing risk-related activities?

666. What are the main aims, objectives of the policy, strategy, or service and the intended outcomes?

667. What is a Community Risk Register?

2.33 Probability and Impact Assessment: Reference Architectures

668. Do the requirements require the creation of new algorithms?

669. What should be done with non-critical risks?

670. Are people attending meetings and doing work?

671. Risks should be identified during which phase of Reference Architectures project management life cycle?

672. How are you working with risks?

673. Are requirements fully understood by the software engineering team and customers?

674. Who will be in command to monitor and control the performance of the consortium members (consortium leader/client)?

675. What is the likelihood?

676. Is the present organizational structure for handling the Reference Architectures project sufficient?

677. How will the consumption pattern change?

678. What are the probabilities of chosen technologies being suitable for local conditions?

679. Are Reference Architectures project requirements stable?

680. What is the level of experience available with your organization?

681. Are the facilities, expertise, resources, and management know-how available to handle the situation?

682. Would avoiding any of corresponding impact the Reference Architectures projects chance of success?

683. What should be the level of coordination?

684. What risks are necessary to achieve success?

685. What are the uncertainties associated with the technology selected for the Reference Architectures project?

686. Is the process supported by tools?

687. How do risks change during a Reference Architectures project life cycle?

2.34 Probability and Impact Matrix: Reference Architectures

688. Who has experience with this?

689. How do you analyze the risks in the different types of Reference Architectures projects?

690. How carefully have the potential competitors been identified?

691. What should you do FIRST?

692. Do you need a risk management plan?

693. What do you expect?

694. What has the Reference Architectures project manager forgotten to do?

695. Non-valid or incredible information?

696. What changes in the regulation are forthcoming?

697. Have staff received necessary training?

698. Is the Reference Architectures project cutting across the entire organization?

699. What will be cost of redeployment of the personnel?

700. How do risks change during the Reference

Architectures projects life cycle?

701. Which risks need to move on to Perform Quantitative Risk Analysis?

702. Prioritized components/features?

703. Are you working on the right risks?

704. How do you manage Reference Architectures project Risk?

2.35 Risk Data Sheet: Reference Architectures

705. What are the main opportunities available to you that you should grab while you can?

706. What if client refuses?

707. Risk of what?

708. What are your core values?

709. How do you handle product safely?

710. What are you trying to achieve (Objectives)?

711. How reliable is the data source?

712. What do you know?

713. Potential for recurrence?

714. What do people affected think about the need for, and practicality of preventive measures?

715. What can happen?

716. What are you here for (Mission)?

717. Who has a vested interest in how you perform as your organization (our stakeholders)?

718. What were the Causes that contributed?

719. Will revised controls lead to tolerable risk levels?

720. Is the data sufficiently specified in terms of the type of failure being analyzed, and its frequency or probability?

721. Has the most cost-effective solution been chosen?

722. What actions can be taken to eliminate or remove risk?

723. Whom do you serve (customers)?

724. How can it happen?

2.36 Procurement Management Plan: Reference Architectures

725. Is there a procurement management plan in place?

726. Is there a formal set of procedures supporting Stakeholder Management?

727. Is the Reference Architectures project sponsor clearly communicating the business case or rationale for why this Reference Architectures project is needed?

728. Do you have the reasons why the changes to your organizational systems and capabilities are required?

729. Is the structure for tracking the Reference Architectures project schedule well defined and assigned to a specific individual?

730. Do Reference Architectures project teams & team members report on status / activities / progress?

731. What types of contracts will be used?

732. Are updated Reference Architectures project time & resource estimates reasonable based on the current Reference Architectures project stage?

733. What is a Reference Architectures project Management Plan?

734. Has the business need been clearly defined?

735. Are changes in scope (deliverable commitments) agreed to by all affected groups & individuals?

736. Are Reference Architectures project contact logs kept up to date?

737. If standardized procurement documents are needed, where can others be found?

738. What are you trying to accomplish?

739. Are mitigation strategies identified?

740. Is it possible to track all classes of Reference Architectures project work (e.g. scheduled, un-scheduled, defect repair, etc.)?

741. Are written status reports provided on a designated frequent basis?

742. Public engagement – did you get it right?

2.37 Source Selection Criteria: Reference Architectures

743. What are the guidelines regarding award without considerations?

744. Do you want to have them collaborate at subfactor level?

745. What should be the contracting officers strategy?

746. Do you ensure you evaluate what you asked for, not what you want to see or expect to see?

747. What is cost analysis and when should it be performed?

748. What risks were identified in the proposals?

749. When should debriefings be held and how should they be scheduled?

750. Is a cost realism analysis used?

751. What are the limitations on pre-competitive range communications?

752. Who is on the Source Selection Advisory Committee?

753. What can not be disclosed?

754. What does a sample rating scale look like?

755. Have all evaluators been trained?

756. What management structure does your organization consider as optimal for performing the contract?

757. What documentation should be used to support the selection decision?

758. How can the methods of publicizing the buy be tailored to yield more effective price competition?

759. Are they compliant with all technical requirements?

760. How much weight should be placed on past performance information?

761. Can you make a cost/technical tradeoff?

762. Is the contracting office likely to receive more purchase requests for this item or service during the coming year?

2.38 Stakeholder Management Plan: Reference Architectures

763. Are best practices and metrics employed to identify issues, progress, performance, etc.?

764. Does the Reference Architectures project have a Statement of Work?

765. Has the schedule been baselined?

766. How accurate and complete is the information?

767. What methods are to be used for managing and monitoring subcontractors (eg agreements, contracts etc)?

768. Are tasks tracked by hours?

769. Does a documented Reference Architectures project organizational policy & plan (i.e. governance model) exist?

770. Were the budget estimates reasonable?

771. Are target dates established for each milestone deliverable?

772. Does all Reference Architectures project documentation reside in a common repository for easy access?

773. How are stakeholders chosen and what roles

might they have on a Reference Architectures project?

774. Are you meeting your customers expectations consistently?

775. Has the Reference Architectures project manager been identified?

776. What proven methodologies and standards will be used to ensure that materials, products, processes and services are fit for purpose?

777. Is it standard practice to formally commit stakeholders to the Reference Architectures project via agreements?

778. What action will be taken once reports have been received?

779. Are decisions captured in a decisions log?

780. Are the key elements of a Reference Architectures project Charter present?

781. Are schedule deliverables actually delivered?

2.39 Change Management Plan: Reference Architectures

782. What new behaviours are required?

783. What are the major changes to processes?

784. Who might present the most resistance?

785. What goal(s) do you hope to accomplish?

786. Will a different work structure focus people on what is important?

787. What are the key change management success metrics?

788. Who should be involved in developing a change management strategy?

789. Do you need new systems?

790. How prevalent is Resistance to Change?

791. What will be the preferred method of delivery?

792. Who might be able to help you the most?

793. What would be an estimate of the total cost for the activities required to carry out the change initiative?

794. Has the training co-ordinator been provided with

the training details and put in place the necessary arrangements?

795. What prerequisite knowledge or training is required?

796. Who will fund the training?

797. What risks may occur upfront?

798. Where will the funds come from?

799. What is going to be done differently?

800. Has the training provider been established?

801. How many people are required in each of the roles?

3.0 Executing Process Group: Reference Architectures

802. What areas does the group agree are the biggest success on the Reference Architectures project?

803. Are decisions made in a timely manner?

804. How does Reference Architectures project management relate to other disciplines?

805. When is the appropriate time to bring the scorecard to Board meetings?

806. What are the Reference Architectures project management deliverables of each process group?

807. Do the partners have sufficient financial capacity to keep up the benefits produced by the programme?

808. What were things that you need to improve?

809. Will outside resources be needed to help?

810. Will new hardware or software be required for servers or client machines?

811. Contingency planning. if a risk event occurs, what will you do?

812. Were sponsors and decision makers available when needed outside regularly scheduled meetings?

813. Do schedule issues conflicts?

814. What is the product of your Reference Architectures project?

815. Is the Reference Architectures project performing better or worse than planned?

816. Does software appear easy to learn?

817. Who are the Reference Architectures project stakeholders?

818. What is the critical path for this Reference Architectures project and how long is it?

819. What is the difference between using brainstorming and the Delphi technique for risk identification?

820. What are the typical Reference Architectures project management skills?

3.1 Team Member Status Report: Reference Architectures

821. How will resource planning be done?

822. Does the product, good, or service already exist within your organization?

823. Are the attitudes of staff regarding Reference Architectures project work improving?

824. What is to be done?

825. The problem with Reward & Recognition Programs is that the truly deserving people all too often get left out. How can you make it practical?

826. Does every department have to have a Reference Architectures project Manager on staff?

827. Does your organization have the means (staff, money, contract, etc.) to produce or to acquire the product, good, or service?

828. How much risk is involved?

829. Do you have an Enterprise Reference Architectures project Management Office (EPMO)?

830. What specific interest groups do you have in place?

831. Why is it to be done?

832. How does this product, good, or service meet the needs of the Reference Architectures project and your organization as a whole?

833. Are the products of your organizations Reference Architectures projects meeting customers objectives?

834. Are your organizations Reference Architectures projects more successful over time?

835. How can you make it practical?

836. How it is to be done?

837. When a teams productivity and success depend on collaboration and the efficient flow of information, what generally fails them?

838. Is there evidence that staff is taking a more professional approach toward management of your organizations Reference Architectures projects?

839. Will the staff do training or is that done by a third party?

3.2 Change Request: Reference Architectures

840. What are the basic mechanics of the Change Advisory Board (CAB)?

841. What kind of information about the change request needs to be captured?

842. What mechanism is used to appraise others of changes that are made?

843. What are the duties of the change control team?

844. What are the requirements for urgent changes?

845. What should be regulated in a change control operating instruction?

846. Is it feasible to use requirements attributes as predictors of reliability?

847. What needs to be communicated?

848. Who needs to approve change requests?

849. Has a formal technical review been conducted to assess technical correctness?

850. Why control change across the life cycle?

851. How to get changes (code) out in a timely manner?

852. How does your organization control changes before and after software is released to a customer?

853. Have all related configuration items been properly updated?

854. Are change requests logged and managed?

855. Who is communicating the change?

856. Who can suggest changes?

857. For which areas does this operating procedure apply?

858. Will all change requests be unconditionally tracked through this process?

3.3 Change Log: Reference Architectures

859. When was the request approved?

860. Is the submitted change a new change or a modification of a previously approved change?

861. Where do changes come from?

862. Who initiated the change request?

863. Should a more thorough impact analysis be conducted?

864. Is the change request within Reference Architectures project scope?

865. Do the described changes impact on the integrity or security of the system?

866. Is the change request open, closed or pending?

867. Is the requested change request a result of changes in other Reference Architectures project(s)?

868. Will the Reference Architectures project fail if the change request is not executed?

869. Is this a mandatory replacement?

870. How does this relate to the standards developed for specific business processes?

871. How does this change affect scope?

872. Is the change backward compatible without limitations?

873. Does the suggested change request represent a desired enhancement to the products functionality?

874. When was the request submitted?

875. How does this change affect the timeline of the schedule?

3.4 Decision Log: Reference Architectures

876. Adversarial environment. is your opponent open to a non-traditional workflow, or will it likely challenge anything you do?

877. What makes you different or better than others companies selling the same thing?

878. Who will be given a copy of this document and where will it be kept?

879. What was the rationale for the decision?

880. Behaviors; what are guidelines that the team has identified that will assist them with getting the most out of team meetings?

881. What are the cost implications?

882. Which variables make a critical difference?

883. How do you know when you are achieving it?

884. How effective is maintaining the log at facilitating organizational learning?

885. How consolidated and comprehensive a story can you tell by capturing currently available incident data in a central location and through a log of key decisions during an incident?

886. How does the use a Decision Support System influence the strategies/tactics or costs?

887. How does an increasing emphasis on cost containment influence the strategies and tactics used?

888. Decision-making process; how will the team make decisions?

889. What eDiscovery problem or issue did your organization set out to fix or make better?

890. Meeting purpose; why does this team meet?

891. It becomes critical to track and periodically revisit both operational effectiveness; Are you noticing all that you need to, and are you interpreting what you see effectively?

892. Does anything need to be adjusted?

893. Is your opponent open to a non-traditional workflow, or will it likely challenge anything you do?

894. At what point in time does loss become unacceptable?

895. How do you define success?

3.5 Quality Audit: Reference Architectures

896. Is there a written corporate quality policy?

897. Are the policies and processes, as set out in the Quality Audit Manual, properly applied?

898. How does your organization know that the range and quality of its social and recreational services and facilities are appropriately effective and constructive in meeting the needs of staff?

899. What are your supplier audits?

900. What happens if your organization fails its Quality Audit?

901. Are measuring and test equipment that have been placed out of service suitably identified and excluded from use in any device reconditioning operation?

902. Are there appropriate means for intervening if necessary?

903. For each device to be reconditioned, are device specifications, such as appropriate engineering drawings, component specifications and software specifications, maintained?

904. Does the suppliers quality system have a written procedure for corrective action when a defect occurs?

905. Are salvageable and salvaged medical devices stored in a manner to prevent damage and/or contamination?

906. How does your organization know that its staff placements are appropriately effective and constructive in relation to program-related learning outcomes?

907. Does everyone know what they are supposed to be doing, how and why?

908. How does your organization know that its promotions system is appropriately effective, constructive and fair?

909. What experience do staff have in the type of work that the audit entails?

910. Are training programs documented?

911. Are people allowed to contribute ideas?

912. How does your organization know that its system for attending to the health and wellbeing of its staff is appropriately effective and constructive?

913. How does your organization know that its systems for meeting staff extracurricular learning support requirements are appropriately effective and constructive?

914. Are the intentions consistent with external obligations (such as applicable laws)?

915. How does the organization know that its system for maintaining and advancing the capabilities of its staff, particularly in relation to the Mission of the organization, is appropriately effective and constructive?

3.6 Team Directory: Reference Architectures

916. Process decisions: do job conditions warrant additional actions to collect job information and document on-site activity?

917. Contract requirements complied with?

918. Does a Reference Architectures project team directory list all resources assigned to the Reference Architectures project?

919. How will you accomplish and manage the objectives?

920. Who will be the stakeholders on your next Reference Architectures project?

921. Who will write the meeting minutes and distribute?

922. Decisions: what could be done better to improve the quality of the constructed product?

923. Where should the information be distributed?

924. Process decisions: which organizational elements and which individuals will be assigned management functions?

925. Decisions: is the most suitable form of contract being used?

926. Timing: when do the effects of communication take place?

927. Process decisions: are there any statutory or regulatory issues relevant to the timely execution of work?

928. Do purchase specifications and configurations match requirements?

929. Is construction on schedule?

930. Process decisions: how well was task order work performed?

931. When will you produce deliverables?

932. How do unidentified risks impact the outcome of the Reference Architectures project?

933. Who are your stakeholders (customers, sponsors, end users, team members)?

934. Days from the time the issue is identified?

3.7 Team Operating Agreement: Reference Architectures

935. What are the current caseload numbers in the unit?

936. Must your members collaborate successfully to complete Reference Architectures projects?

937. Methodologies: how will key team processes be implemented, such as training, research, work deliverable production, review and approval processes, knowledge management, and meeting procedures?

938. What is the number of cases currently teamed?

939. Do you solicit member feedback about meetings and what would make them better?

940. Conflict resolution: how will disputes and other conflicts be mediated or resolved?

941. Do you begin with a question to engage everyone?

942. Have you established procedures that team members can follow to work effectively together, such as a team operating agreement?

943. Do you send out the agenda and meeting materials in advance?

944. Reimbursements: how will the team members be reimbursed for expenses and time commitments?

945. Must your team members rely on the expertise of other members to complete tasks?

946. Did you recap the meeting purpose, time, and expectations?

947. Did you determine the technology methods that best match the messages to be communicated?

948. What is group supervision?

949. Does your team need access to all documents and information at all times?

950. Seconds for members to respond?

951. Are there differences in access to communication and collaboration technology based on team member location?

952. Do you ask participants to close laptops and place mobile devices on silent on the table while the meeting is in progress?

953. Is compensation based on team and individual performance?

954. Do you post meeting notes and the recording (if used) and notify participants?

3.8 Team Performance Assessment: Reference Architectures

955. How hard did you try to make a good selection?

956. To what degree do members understand and articulate the same purpose without relying on ambiguous abstractions?

957. To what degree can the team ensure that all members are individually and jointly accountable for the teams purpose, goals, approach, and work-products?

958. How do you manage human resources?

959. How do you encourage members to learn from each other?

960. If you have criticized someones work for method variance in your role as reviewer, what was the circumstance?

961. To what degree are the goals realistic?

962. To what degree will the team adopt a concrete, clearly understood, and agreed-upon approach that will result in achievement of the teams goals?

963. To what degree can the team measure progress against specific goals?

964. To what degree can all members engage in open

and interactive considerations?

965. To what degree does the teams work approach provide opportunity for members to engage in fact-based problem solving?

966. Is there a particular method of data analysis that you would recommend as a means of demonstrating that method variance is not of great concern for a given dataset?

967. To what degree will team members, individually and collectively, commit time to help themselves and others learn and develop skills?

968. To what degree do all members feel responsible for all agreed-upon measures?

969. Effects of crew composition on crew performance: Does the whole equal the sum of its parts?

970. To what degree do team members articulate the teams work approach?

971. To what degree do the goals specify concrete team work products?

972. Can team performance be reliably measured in simulator and live exercises using the same assessment tool?

973. To what degree will the approach capitalize on and enhance the skills of all team members in a manner that takes into consideration other demands on members of the team?

974. To what degree is the team cognizant of small wins to be celebrated along the way?

3.9 Team Member Performance Assessment: Reference Architectures

975. What are top priorities?

976. Has the appropriate access to relevant data and analysis capability been granted?

977. What changes do you need to make to align practices with beliefs?

978. Why were corresponding selected?

979. What is needed for effective data teams?

980. What does collaboration look like?

981. What qualities does a successful Team leader possess?

982. Are any validation activities performed?

983. How will they be formed?

984. How are evaluation results utilized?

985. How often are assessments to be conducted?

986. How are training activities developed from a technical perspective?

987. How do you implement Cost Reduction?

988. Goals met?

989. How do you make use of research?

990. How is performance assessment used in making future award decisions including options and extend/compete decisions?

991. What is the large, desired outcome?

992. What is collaboration?

993. What are best practices for delivering and developing training evaluations to maximize the benefits of leveraging emerging technologies?

3.10 Issue Log: Reference Architectures

994. How do you reply to this question; you am new here and managing this major program. How do you suggest you build your network?

995. Do you have members of your team responsible for certain stakeholders?

996. In classifying stakeholders, which approach to do so are you using?

997. What is the impact on the Business Case?

998. Why not more evaluators?

999. Is the issue log kept in a safe place?

1000. In your work, how much time is spent on stakeholder identification?

1001. Are there too many who have an interest in some aspect of your work?

1002. Which stakeholders can influence others?

1003. Do you feel a register helps?

1004. What is the stakeholders political influence?

1005. Which team member will work with each stakeholder?

1006. Why do you manage human resources?

1007. Who do you turn to if you have questions?

1008. What is a Stakeholder?

1009. Who have you worked with in past, similar initiatives?

4.0 Monitoring and Controlling Process Group: Reference Architectures

1010. How is agile Reference Architectures project management done?

1011. What will you do to minimize the impact should a risk event occur?

1012. Do clients benefit (change) from the services?

1013. What business situation is being addressed?

1014. Is there undesirable impact on staff or resources?

1015. Use: how will they use the information?

1016. What is the timeline for the Reference Architectures project?

1017. Is the program in place as intended?

1018. User: who wants the information and what are they interested in?

1019. Where is the Risk in the Reference Architectures project?

1020. How can you monitor progress?

1021. How well defined and documented were

the Reference Architectures project management processes you chose to use?

1022. Purpose: toward what end is the evaluation being conducted?

1023. Who needs to be involved in the planning?

1024. Key stakeholders to work with. How many potential communications channels exist on the Reference Architectures project?

1025. How is Agile Reference Architectures project Management done?

1026. Is it what was agreed upon?

1027. Were escalated issues resolved promptly?

1028. How many more potential communications channels were introduced by the discovery of the new stakeholders?

4.1 Project Performance Report: Reference Architectures

1029. To what degree do team members feel that the purpose of the team is important, if not exciting?

1030. To what degree does the information network provide individuals with the information they require?

1031. To what degree does the teams work approach provide opportunity for members to engage in open interaction?

1032. What is the PRS?

1033. To what degree are the structures of the formal organization consistent with the behaviors in the informal organization?

1034. How will procurement be coordinated with other Reference Architectures project aspects, such as scheduling and performance reporting?

1035. To what degree does the teams purpose contain themes that are particularly meaningful and memorable?

1036. To what degree are the tasks requirements reflected in the flow and storage of information?

1037. To what degree is there a sense that only the team can succeed?

1038. To what degree are the demands of the task compatible with and converge with the relationships of the informal organization?

1039. What is in it for you?

1040. To what degree does the formal organization make use of individual resources and meet individual needs?

1041. To what degree are fresh input and perspectives systematically caught and added (for example, through information and analysis, new members, and senior sponsors)?

1042. To what degree will the team ensure that all members equitably share the work essential to the success of the team?

1043. To what degree can team members meet frequently enough to accomplish the teams ends?

1044. To what degree will new and supplemental skills be introduced as the need is recognized?

1045. To what degree do team members frequently explore the teams purpose and its implications?

1046. What is the degree to which rules govern information exchange between individuals within your organization?

4.2 Variance Analysis: Reference Architectures

1047. Are records maintained to show how management reserves are used?

1048. There are detailed schedules which support control account and work package start and completion dates/events?

1049. What is the expected future profitability of each customer?

1050. Is the market likely to continue to grow at this rate next year?

1051. How do you identify and isolate causes of favorable and unfavorable cost and schedule variances?

1052. What is the incurrence of actual indirect costs in excess of budgets, by element of expense?

1053. Do the rates and prices remain constant throughout the year?

1054. How does the monthly budget compare to the actual experience?

1055. Are there knowledgeable Reference Architectures projections of future performance?

1056. What causes selling price variance?

1057. Is data disseminated to the contractors management timely, accurate, and usable?

1058. What business event causes fluctuations?

1059. Wbs elements contractually specified for reporting of status to your organization (lowest level only)?

1060. Are your organizations and items of cost assigned to each pool identified?

1061. Are control accounts opened and closed based on the start and completion of work contained therein?

1062. Did your organization lose existing customers and/or gain new customers?

1063. What can be the cause of an increase in costs?

1064. What should management do?

1065. How does the use of a single conversion element (rather than the traditional labor and overhead elements) affect standard costing?

4.3 Earned Value Status: Reference Architectures

1066. Earned value can be used in almost any Reference Architectures project situation and in almost any Reference Architectures project environment. it may be used on large Reference Architectures projects, medium sized Reference Architectures projects, tiny Reference Architectures projects (in cut-down form), complex and simple Reference Architectures projects and in any market sector. some people, of course, know all about earned value, they have used it for years - but perhaps not as effectively as they could have?

1067. Validation is a process of ensuring that the developed system will actually achieve the stakeholders desired outcomes; Are you building the right product? What do you validate?

1068. If earned value management (EVM) is so good in determining the true status of a Reference Architectures project and Reference Architectures project its completion, why is it that hardly any one uses it in information systems related Reference Architectures projects?

1069. What is the unit of forecast value?

1070. Where is evidence-based earned value in your organization reported?

1071. Where are your problem areas?

1072. Are you hitting your Reference Architectures projects targets?

1073. Verification is a process of ensuring that the developed system satisfies the stakeholders agreements and specifications; Are you building the product right? What do you verify?

1074. How does this compare with other Reference Architectures projects?

1075. When is it going to finish?

1076. How much is it going to cost by the finish?

4.4 Risk Audit: Reference Architectures

1077. Do you ensure the recommended rules of play and protocols are followed for your activity?

1078. Is the number of people on the Reference Architectures project team adequate to do the job?

1079. Number of users of the product?

1080. How risk averse are you?

1081. How do you prioritize risks?

1082. Are procedures developed to respond to foreseeable emergencies and communicated to all involved?

1083. What are the differences and similarities between strategic and operational risks in your organization?

1084. Will participants be required to sign a legally counselled waiver or risk disclaimer when entering an event?

1085. Does your board meet regularly and document all decisions and actions?

1086. What are the risks that could stop you from achieving your objectives?

1087. Will an appropriate standard of care be applied to all involved?

1088. Does the customer understand the process?

1089. Are corresponding safety and risk management policies posted for all to see?

1090. How will you maximise opportunities?

1091. Do you have position descriptions for all office bearers/staff?

1092. Does the team have the right mix of skills?

1093. Does your organization meet the terms of any contracts with which it is involved?

1094. Improving fraud detection: do auditors react to abnormal inconsistencies between financial and non-financial measures?

1095. If applicable; does the software interface with new or unproven hardware or unproven vendor products?

1096. Are tools for analysis and design available?

4.5 Contractor Status Report: Reference Architectures

1097. Who can list a Reference Architectures project as organization experience, your organization or a previous employee of your organization?

1098. How does the proposed individual meet each requirement?

1099. How long have you been using the services?

1100. If applicable; describe your standard schedule for new software version releases. Are new software version releases included in the standard maintenance plan?

1101. What was the final actual cost?

1102. What was the actual budget or estimated cost for your organizations services?

1103. Are there contractual transfer concerns?

1104. What is the average response time for answering a support call?

1105. How is risk transferred?

1106. What was the budget or estimated cost for your organizations services?

1107. What process manages the contracts?

1108. Describe how often regular updates are made to the proposed solution. Are corresponding regular updates included in the standard maintenance plan?

1109. What are the minimum and optimal bandwidth requirements for the proposed solution?

1110. What was the overall budget or estimated cost?

4.6 Formal Acceptance: Reference Architectures

1111. What is the Acceptance Management Process?

1112. Who supplies data?

1113. Was the client satisfied with the Reference Architectures project results?

1114. What was done right?

1115. Have all comments been addressed?

1116. Did the Reference Architectures project manager and team act in a professional and ethical manner?

1117. Was the Reference Architectures project managed well?

1118. Is formal acceptance of the Reference Architectures project product documented and distributed?

1119. Do you perform formal acceptance or burn-in tests?

1120. General estimate of the costs and times to complete the Reference Architectures project?

1121. Do you buy-in installation services?

1122. Do you buy pre-configured systems or build your own configuration?

1123. Was the Reference Architectures project work done on time, within budget, and according to specification?

1124. Was the sponsor/customer satisfied?

1125. Did the Reference Architectures project achieve its MOV?

1126. What can you do better next time?

1127. How well did the team follow the methodology?

1128. What are the requirements against which to test, Who will execute?

1129. What lessons were learned about your Reference Architectures project management methodology?

1130. Does it do what client said it would?

5.0 Closing Process Group: Reference Architectures

1131. Is the Reference Architectures project funded?

1132. How critical is the Reference Architectures project success to the success of your organization?

1133. Just how important is your work to the overall success of the Reference Architectures project?

1134. Measurable - are the targets measurable?

1135. What is the risk of failure to your organization?

1136. How will you do it?

1137. Did the Reference Architectures project team have enough people to execute the Reference Architectures project plan?

1138. What areas does the group agree are the biggest success on the Reference Architectures project?

1139. Did you do what you said you were going to do?

1140. What is the amount of funding and what Reference Architectures project phases are funded?

1141. How well did the chosen processes fit the needs of the Reference Architectures project?

1142. Are there funding or time constraints?

1143. What was learned?

1144. What were the actual outcomes?

1145. What is the overall risk of the Reference Architectures project to your organization?

1146. What is an Encumbrance?

1147. Did the Reference Architectures project team have the right skills?

5.1 Procurement Audit: Reference Architectures

1148. Does the cash disbursement policy prohibit drawing checks to cash or bearer?

1149. Are incentives to deliver on time and in quantity properly specified?

1150. Were the documents received scrutinised for completion and adherence to stated conditions before the tenders were evaluated?

1151. Do contracts contain regular reviews, targets and quality standards in order to assess suppliers performance?

1152. Were exclusion causes duly considered before the actual evaluation of tenders?

1153. Are approval limits definitive as to amount and classification of expenditure?

1154. Are purchasing actions processed on a timely basis?

1155. Is electronic procurement applied to reduce transaction costs?

1156. Is data securely stored?

1157. Are there systems for recording and monitoring in order to discover malpractice and fraud in the procurement function/unit?

1158. Has the award included no items different from the already stated contained in bid specifications?

1159. Was a sufficient competitive environment created?

1160. Are purchase requisitions used to generate purchase orders?

1161. Are requisitions and other purchase requests batched to reduce the number of orders issued?

1162. Are vendor price lists regularly updated?

1163. Is there time waste during tendering?

1164. Are fixed asset accounts posted currently?

1165. Have guidelines incorporating the principles and objectives of a robust procurement practice been established?

1166. Does the procurement unit have sound commercial awareness and knowledge of suppliers and the market?

1167. Does the individual having check-signing responsibility review the use of the signature plates?

5.2 Contract Close-Out: Reference Architectures

1168. Was the contract type appropriate?

1169. Change in attitude or behavior?

1170. Change in knowledge?

1171. Was the contract complete without requiring numerous changes and revisions?

1172. Have all contract records been included in the Reference Architectures project archives?

1173. Have all acceptance criteria been met prior to final payment to contractors?

1174. What is capture management?

1175. Change in circumstances?

1176. Are the signers the authorized officials?

1177. What happens to the recipient of services?

1178. How does it work?

1179. Parties: Authorized?

1180. Was the contract sufficiently clear so as not to result in numerous disputes and misunderstandings?

1181. Have all contracts been completed?

1182. How is the contracting office notified of the automatic contract close-out?

1183. How/when used ?

1184. Parties: who is involved?

1185. Have all contracts been closed?

1186. Has each contract been audited to verify acceptance and delivery?

5.3 Project or Phase Close-Out: Reference Architectures

1187. What hierarchical authority does the stakeholder have in your organization?

1188. What was the preferred delivery mechanism?

1189. If you were the Reference Architectures project sponsor, how would you determine which Reference Architectures project team(s) and/or individuals deserve recognition?

1190. Did the delivered product meet the specified requirements and goals of the Reference Architectures project?

1191. Does the lesson educate others to improve performance?

1192. Did the Reference Architectures project management methodology work?

1193. Planned completion date?

1194. What is a Risk?

1195. Complete yes or no?

1196. What were the goals and objectives of the communications strategy for the Reference Architectures project?

1197. What advantages do the an individual interview have over a group meeting, and vice-versa?

1198. Is the lesson based on actual Reference Architectures project experience rather than on independent research?

1199. What is this stakeholder expecting?

1200. What security considerations needed to be addressed during the procurement life cycle?

1201. Were cost budgets met?

1202. How much influence did the stakeholder have over others?

1203. Can the lesson learned be replicated?

1204. Planned remaining costs?

5.4 Lessons Learned: Reference Architectures

1205. How effective was the support you received during implementation of the product/service?

1206. How effective were the techniques used to prepare you and your organization for the impact of the changes brought about by the product or service produced by the Reference Architectures project?

1207. How efficient were Reference Architectures project team meetings conducted?

1208. What on the Reference Architectures project worked well and was effective in the delivery of the product?

1209. How many government and contractor personnel are authorized for the Reference Architectures project?

1210. What are the funding priorities for intelligence?

1211. Who managed most of the communication within the Reference Architectures project?

1212. Are there any hidden conflicts of interest?

1213. How well were expectations met regarding the frequency and content of information that was conveyed to by the Reference Architectures project Manager?

1214. What policy constraints are relevant?

1215. What are the performance measures?

1216. How well were your expectations met regarding the extent of your involvement in the Reference Architectures project (effort, time commitments, etc.)?

1217. What mistakes did you successfully avoid making?

1218. How often did you violate the rules?

1219. What were the success factors?

1220. How adequately involved did you feel in Reference Architectures project decisions?

1221. How smooth do you feel Integration has been?

1222. How well prepared were you to receive Reference Architectures project deliverables?

1223. How well did the scope of the Reference Architectures project match what was defined in the Reference Architectures project Proposal?

1224. How well does the product or service the Reference Architectures project produced meet your needs?

Index

replace   56, 128
replicated   257
Report 5-6, 77, 91, 204, 214, 238, 246
reported   151, 242
reporting   68, 100, 115, 136, 138, 151, 194, 238, 241
reports 51, 103, 129, 150, 174, 194, 205, 209
repository   152, 208
represent   76, 178, 219
reproduced   1
reputation   118
request   5, 59, 139, 178, 216, 218-219
requested   1, 83, 218
requests   207, 216-217, 253
require 36, 50, 61, 67, 92, 96, 162, 171, 198, 238
required   20, 31, 34-35, 37, 42, 52, 59, 61, 77-78, 91, 155-156, 171, 183, 188, 194-195, 204, 210-212, 244
requiring   129, 254
research   23, 118, 227, 233, 257
Reserve   174
reserved   1
reserves   152, 240
reside 75, 208
Resistance   210
resolution   64, 75, 192, 227
resolve 20, 22, 157
resolved   137, 195, 227, 237
resource   3-4, 110, 137, 152, 157, 162, 164, 172, 190, 204, 214
resources   2, 7, 17, 20, 22, 28, 31, 44, 62, 77, 91-92, 101, 106, 110, 116, 130-131, 145, 155-157, 164, 166, 174, 176, 179, 199, 212, 225, 229, 235-236, 239
respect   1
respond   228, 244
responded   11
responding   196
response   16, 23, 91-93, 95, 100, 246
responses   87, 197
responsive   168, 176
result 76, 81, 174, 176, 178, 180, 183, 218, 229, 254
resulted   95
resulting   72, 144
results 8, 37-38, 68, 74, 76-79, 83, 85, 87, 91, 96, 133, 156, 177, 182, 232, 248

standards   1, 9-10, 94-95, 97-98, 100, 209, 218, 252
started 8, 158
starting9
starts   132
stated 114-115, 140, 183, 252-253
statement   3, 10, 82, 144-145, 174, 178, 208
statements   11, 25, 36, 41-42, 57, 73, 89, 101, 123, 184
status 5-6, 126, 136, 151-152, 190, 204-205, 214, 241-242, 246
statutory   226
steady 45
steering   146, 172, 190
storage   184, 238
stored 223, 252
stories 37
strategic   96, 115, 137, 181, 244
strategies   82, 98, 104, 110, 145, 194, 205, 221
strategy   25, 35, 56, 76, 85, 91, 106, 116, 122, 197, 206, 210,
256
Stream 59, 68
strengths   146, 158
stretch 103
strive   103
striving 128
strong 188
Strongly   10, 15, 27, 43, 58, 74, 90, 102
structure   3-4, 52, 86, 114, 144, 148-149, 164, 171, 198, 204,
207, 210
Structured   119
structures   238
stubborn   113
stupid 115
subfactor   206
subject8-9, 34
subjects   65
submitted   218-219
subset 24
succeed   47, 158, 238
success   16, 23, 34, 36, 40, 48, 50, 56, 80, 87, 105, 107-108,
114, 116, 125, 160, 199, 210, 212, 215, 221, 239, 250, 259
successes   120
successful   60, 82, 100, 107, 125, 133, 164, 192, 215, 232
succession   93
suddenly   195

CPSIA information can be obtained
at www.ICGtesting.com
Printed in the USA
BVHW082017110819
555624BV00016BA/2003/P

9 780655 832829